Behind
COMMUNISM

By Frank L. Britton

1708 Patterson Road • Austin, Texas 78733

Behind Communism

Revised Edition

Copyright © 1953, by Frank Britton. Update by Lawrence Patterson, *Criminal Politics* magazine, 1994. Published by RiverCrest Publishing, 1708 Patterson Road, Austin, Texas 78733 in 2014.

The publisher has taken great care to abide by copyright law in preparing this book. Please notify the publisher of any inadvertent omission, and correction will be made at the earliest opportunity. Photos and illustrations and the rights thereto remain the property of the original sources and are used here only as provided by USA copyright law.

Printed in the United States of America

Library of Congress Catalog Card Number 2014937302
Categories: 1.   Religion   2.   Judaism
              3.   Political Science   4.   History

ISBN 978-1-930004-86-3

FOREWORD

JUDAISM IS COMMUNISM

Jews around the world celebrated in 1917 when the Bolsheviks (Communists), led by Lenin and Trotsky, seized power in Moscow. They noted that the first legislative act passed by the new legislature was the *"Anti-Semitism Act."* This law made it a criminal offense to defame Jews and Judaism. Even a joke about the Jews was classified as a hate crime punishable by ten years in prison.

Jews from America, Europe, and across the globe poured in to Russia and its captive republics. The victory in Russia, they believed, validated the Talmud, their holy law, and these Jews wanted to be part of the great Jewish success.

In America particularly, Jews everywhere were ecstatic. Rabbi Harry Wator, in his book, *A Program for the Jews and Humanity,* stated:

"The Communist soul is the soul of Judaism. Hence it follows that in the Russian revolution, the triumph of Communism was the triumph of Judaism..."

Of course, the Jews quickly murdered the captured Russian Czar and his entire family. The murder of the Czar was a signal to the Jews in Russia that the bloodbath had begun in earnest. From that point on, the horrors grew and grew. Russia was soaked in blood.

Robert Wilton, a longtime Russian news correspondent for the *London Times,* said in his book, *The Last Days of the Romanovs*:

"Out of 556 important functionaries of the Bolshevik State, there were, in 1918-1919, 17 Russians... 457 Jews, and 82 others."

Lenin, according to the Lenin Museum on Red Square in Moscow, was a Jew. His deputy, the bloody and cunning Leon Trotsky, was a Jew, and everywhere Jewish commissars were put in charge. Aleksandr Solzhenitsyn, in his classic history text, *Two Hundred Years Together*, noted that even the commandants of the Soviet gulag camps were predominantly Jewish and most were rabbis.

Solzhenitsyn's sources recorded a staggering 66 million were victims of the communists. Churches were burned or turned into barns and brothels. Ministers and priests were taken to the gulag.

The Jews were convinced that their "God," whom Jesus Christ identified in Scripture as the "Devil," had given them the huge empire of the Soviet Union as only the first conquest in a coming string of global victories. The Talmud promises the Jew a Jewish Utopia. The entire world and all its non-Jewish peoples are destined to serve as slaves for the supposedly superior Jews, says the Talmud.

The communists claimed that they were atheists. However, the tribal brainwashing of Judaism and the beliefs of the Jews that in the Talmud is an accurate forecast of the Jewish future made minds of the atheists a fertile ground for the propaganda of Judaism. In fact, communism is simply an outgrowth of Zionism. Zionism and communism are ideological heirs of the Judaic doctrines.

The American Hebrew, September 10, 1920, bragged of this success:

"The Bolshevist revolution in Russia was the work of Jewish brains, of Jewish dissatisfaction, of Jewish planning, whose goal is to create a new order in the world. What was performed in so excellent a way in Russia, due to Jewish brains and because of Jewish dissatisfaction, and by Jewish planning, shall also, through the same Jewish mental and physical forces, became a reality all over the world."

At the time, the Jews in Russia made up only 1.5 percent of the total population. *One and one-half percent!* By cunning lies and manipulation and thanks to the money of Jewish bankers in Germany, Britain, and the United States, Russia fell, and Satan was able to do his dirty work.

Today, in the United States, we have about 2.5 percent of the population that is Jewish. But the same forces are at work to destroy this nation. The parasitical Jews are using the U.S. as proxy to conquer the Middle East. They have in their sights a new world order. The Jewish neocons, aided in their immense crimes by the deceived and naïve Christian Zionists, will, if they have their way, do to America what Lenin, Trotsky, and Stalin did to the vast Soviet Empire.

In 1920, Sir Winston Churchill, who later became Great Britain's leader in World War II, wrote an editorial in the *Illustrated Sunday Herald of London*. He warned of a "worldwide revolutionary conspiracy for the overthrow of civilization and for the reconstitution of society on the basis of arrested development (and) envious malevolence."

Churchill wrote that the Jewish subversives have played:

"...a definite recognizable part in the tragedy of the French Revolution. It has been the mainspring of every subversive movement during the nineteenth century; and now at last this band of extraordinary personalities from the great cities of Europe and America have gripped the Russian people by the hair of their head and have become practically the undisputed masters of the enormous empire."

In 1935, the most famous rabbi in America, Rabbi Stephen Wise, a friend of President Roosevelt, boasted: "Some call it Marxism. I call it Judaism." (*The American Bulletin*, May 5, 1935)

Fast-forward to Russia, under President Putin. In June 2013, in a courageous speech before the Jewish and Tolerance Center in Moscow, Putin shocked the assembled Jewish guests by stating what the so-called "free press" of the West had covered up and censored for almost a century.

"The decision to nationalize this library (in 1917) was made by the first Soviet Government, whose composition was 80-85 percent Jewish. These government bureaucrats were guided by ideological considerations and supported... arrest and suppression."

This book, *Behind Communism*, by Frank Britton, further elaborates on the astute knowledge held by Winston Churchill, Vladimir Putin, and others who have studied world history. It explains *who* Karl Marx was—he was the grandson of a Jewish rabbi. It reveals how a small band of Jewish criminals, masterminded by Jewish bankers in New York and Germany, took over one of the world's greatest empires.

The Jews founded a monstrous *pathocracy* in Soviet Russia. A pathocracy is a nation run by a minority who are *psychopaths*. These psychopaths were, in fact, serial killers, much like American criminals Ted Bundy, Jeffrey Dahmer, and Henry Lee Lucas. These men do not think like you and I, and they had neither empathy nor remorse. They used the religion of Judaism and the ideology of Communism as tools for plunder and death, convenient strategies that disguised their murderous pathology.

It is the Jewish Talmud that forms the basis of this deadly pathology. The Kabbala assists in its formation. Today, the Jews continue to be led by madmen who use Judaism, Zionism, and the "Chosen People" myth as tools to deceive and manipulate. These evil men and women are determined to rule the earth, and they intend to murder most of its non-Jewish inhabitants.

Sixty-six million died in the communist era in Russia. The Jewish ideology was responsible for tens of millions more deaths in China and in Eastern Europe. We must understand the past in order to insure a safe and secure future. Unless the dangerous and wicked religion and political ideology of the Jew and its revolutionary and racist doctrines are exposed, we will surely be forced to endure a horrible repeat of this dark period.

I firmly believe that this book, *Behind Communism*, is a great contribution to understanding the past. Let us use this knowledge, then, to guide us into future light.

— Texe Marrs
Austin, Texas

THE PERSECUTION MYTH

With Shrill Insistence

We cannot undertake even this brief history of the modern Jew without taking note of a phenomenon which has confounded gentile societies for twenty centuries. This is the ability of the Jewish people to collectively retain their identity despite centuries of exposure to Christian civilization. To any student of Judaism, or to the Jews themselves, this phenomenon is partly explained by the fact that Judaism is neither mainly a religion nor mainly a racial matter, nor yet is it simply a matter of nationality. Rather it is all three; it is a kind of trinity. Judaism is best described as a nationality built on the twin pillars of race and religion.

All this is closely related to another aspect of Judaism, namely, the persecution myth. Since first appearing in history we find the Jews propagating the idea that they are an abused and persecuted people, and this idea is, and has always been, central in Jewish thinking. The myth of persecution is the adhesive and cement of Judaism; without it Jews would have long since ceased to exist, their racial-religious nationality notwithstanding.

Jews do not always agree among themselves, and it is only in the presence of their enemies—real or imagined—that Jewish thinking crystallizes into unanimity. In this respect they differ not at all from other peoples: Adolf Hitler solidified German opinion around the idea that Germany was wronged at Versailles, that the German people were abused and victimized by the Allies, and that only by holding together could they prevail against the overwhelming might of their enemies...

For twenty-five centuries the Jewish mind has been conditioned by the same appeal. Through all Jewish thinking and all Jewish history the refrain of persecution has sounded with shrill insistence. Thus we find every accident of fortune being chronicled, enhanced, and passed on to succeeding generations as another example of gentile cruelty to the chosen race. And almost inevitably we find opposition to Jewish aspirations and ambitions being translated into these same terms of persecution, and all Jewish shortcomings being excused on the same basis.

Now it is a fact that the Jewish people have suffered numerous hardships in the course of their history, but this is true of other peoples too. The chief difference is that the Jews have kept score—they have made a tradition of persecution. A casual slaughter of Christians is remembered by no one in 50 years, but a disability visited upon a few Jews is preserved forever in Jewish histories. And they tell their woes not only to themselves, but to a sympathetic world as well...

THE JEW IN EUROPE
Even The Coins Were Jewish

We find the first Jews filtering into Europe some time before the Christian era, particularly in the region of Greece. The ancient Greeks spoke of these Asiatic invaders with considerable bitterness. Very quickly they spread throughout the Roman Empire and into Europe proper. The Jewish merchant, artisan, and slave trader appear on the Roman scene with increasing frequency after the second century A.D. and there can be no doubt that their position in the Roman world was one of growing importance even as the Empire drifted to destruction. Under Justinian, says the Jewish Encyclopedia, **"They enjoyed full religious liberty, in return for which they assumed all a citizen's duty toward the state; minor offices were also open to them. Only the synagogues were exempt from the duty of quartering soldiers. The trade in slaves constituted the main source of livelihood for the Roman Jews, and decrees against this traffic were issued in 335, 336, 339, 384, etc."**[1]

Seneca, in his writings, bitterly assailed the Romans of his

---

[1] Funk & Wagnall's Jewish Encyclopedia, page 460, vol. 10
NOTE: The FUNK & WAGNALL JEWISH ENCYCLOPEDIA (see preceding page) is uniformly referred to throughout this work as the "Jewish Encyclopedia." Consisting of 12 volumes, it is available in all major libraries. It should not be confused with the 10 volume "Universal Jewish Encylopedia," published by Universal Jewish Encyclopedia, Inc., New York, 1939. Both, however, are authoritative Jewish publications, complied by and for Jews.

BEHIND COMMUNISM ○ 9

Jewish catacombs in Rome dating from the second century A.D.

day for aping the Jews, and some historians (notably Gibbon in his monumental Decline and Fall of the Roman Empire) have ascribed the downfall of Rome to their corrupting influence. Nero's wife, Poppaea, was a converted Jewess.

As Rome reeled into decline and final collapse, and as the Dark Ages descended over Western civilization, we find the Jew taking a strangle-hold over what remained of European commerce. Says Encyclopedia Britannica[2]: "...there was an inevitable tendency for him to specialize in commerce, for which his acumen and ubiquity gave him special qualifications. In the dark ages the commerce of western Europe was largely in his hands, in particular the slave trade. and in Carolingian cartularies Jew and merchant are used as almost interchangeable terms." This hold over European commerce finally became so utterly complete that few gentiles engaged in trade at all; it had become almost entirely a Jewish monopoly. In Poland and Hungary, the coins bore Jewish inscriptions...

Throughout the Medieval period, ["Dark Ages," "Medieval Period," and "Middle Ages" are synonymous terms used to describe the period of decline which characterized western civilization between 500-1300 A.D.] which lasted from 500 A.D. to 1300 A.D., the Jew merchant was dominant all over

---

[2] Encyclopedia Britannica, page 57, vol. 13—1947
NOTE: Encyclopedia Britannica is used as a reference source because of its ready availability to the average reader. It is not an "anti-Semitic publication. In fact, the Encyclopedia Britannica Corporation was purchased by the Julius Rosenwald interests in 1920, and since then all material pertaining to the Jewish question has been re-written to conform to the Jewish outlook.

Europe (except Scandinavia, where he was never permitted to enter) and this dominance included control over the eastern trade routes to the Levant. There was to be no relief from this situation until the Jews were evicted from Europe in the century directly preceding the Renaissance.

In 1215 the Catholic Church, at the Fourth Lateran Council, broke the back of European Jewry with a set of restrictions designed to curb their commercial monopoly. These decrees restricted Jews to residence in their own communities, prohibited absolutely their hiring of Christian employees and prohibited them from engaging in many types of commercial activity.

Expelled

The Fourth Lateran Council restricted Jewish commercial advantage but it did not end the Jewish problem. Beginning in the latter part of the 13th century, one European country after another expelled its Jewish population as the only final solution to the problem. First to take the step was England which banned them in 1290. Fifteen years later in 1306 the French followed suit. In steady succession the various states of Europe emulated this example with Spain being one of the last to enforce the ban in 1492. The situation in Spain is worth noting. Says Encyclopedia Britannica[3]: "**...The 14th century was the golden age of their history in Spain. In 1391 the preaching of a priest of Seville, Fernando Martenez, led to the first general massacre of the Jews who were envied for their prosperity and hated because they were the king's tax collectors.**" Ferdinand and Isabella, after uniting Spain and driving out the Moors turned their attention to the Jewish problem, with the result that they were evicted completely in 1492. In 1498 Portugal evicted its Jewish population also.

The Exploiters

A great deal has been said about the "persecution" of the Jews in Europe and elsewhere, and they have pretty well convinced the world (or at least Americans) that these hardships were inflicted on an innocent people. But these rich

---
3 Encyclopedia Brittanica, page 57, vol. 13 - 1947

Spanish Jews we see being evicted in 1492 were not downtrodden folk. They were the wealthy, the privileged, the exploiters: they were the well-fed merchants and the gouging tax collectors...

So it was in Portugal; in that country we find that the deportation of the Jews... **"deprived Portugal of its middle class and its most scientific traders and financiers."**[4] Undeniably this class of traders and financiers was put to hardship by this banishment, but it does not follow that they were victims of discrimination in the accepted sense, nor were they underprivileged in any way. Rather we see a wealthy merchant group being ousted from its seat of vested privilege by a thoroughly outraged, and a thoroughly exploited Christian society...

The situation in England was similar. The Jews had come to England in the wake of the Norman conquest and had quickly gained a position of wealth and prosperity. Says Valentine's Jewish Encyclopedia of this period: **"Their numbers and prosperity increased, Aaron of Lincoln being the wealthiest man in England in his time... his financial transactions covering the whole country and concerning many of the leading nobles and churchmen... On his death his property passed to the crown and a special branch of the exchequer had to be created to deal with it."**

England

England, ironically enough, was the last country to be invaded by the Jews and the first to evict them. After the Fourth Lateran Council the Jews had become increasingly difficult to deal

Home of Aaron of Lincoln, dating from the 13th century. In his day, Aaron was richer than any prince or nobleman in England. Edward I, conqueror of Wales and one of England's great monarchs, evicted the Jews because they were monopolizing England's wealth.

---
4 Encyclopedia Britannica, page 279, vol. 18—1947

with and there were a number of anti-Jewish riots. Perplexed by the problem posed by this alien minority which seemed well on its way to corralling the kingdom's wealth, and failing in an attempt to force its assimilation. Edward I confiscated all Jewish wealth and evicted them permanently in 1290. Not until 1655 was a Jew legally permitted to re-enter England. Britain thus established the precedent for the later eviction which soon followed on the continent.

France

In France too the Jews were dominant in trade and finance and had been since before Charlemagne's time. Under Philip the Fair (1285-1314) one of the last, and certainly one of the greatest of the Capetian line, France had become the greatest power in Europe. It was Philip's need for money which led him to seize Jewish wealth and drive them from the country. He had already before 1306 taken desperate measures to raise money, which was in short supply, by forbidding the export of gold and silver from France. The same need for money brought him into conflict with the Templars, whose wealth he also seized. But it was the Jews who controlled the greatest supply of floating wealth. In 1306 Philip solved his financial problem—and France's Jewish problem—by expropriating their wealth and evicting them. Thus ended the centuries-long commercial dominance of the Jew in France. Later a few were permitted to return and these were in turn ejected in 1394.

RETURN TO THE EAST

The Evictions

Space does not permit a detailed discussion of the other evictions which followed and which resulted in the banishment of the Jews from virtually every country in Western Europe in the succeeding centuries but here in chronological order is a list of the evictions:

ENGLAND: Jews expelled in 1290 by Edward I. Not permitted to re-enter till 1655.

FRANCE: Expelled in 1306 by Philip the Fair. A few were permitted to return but were again evicted in 1394. Jewish settlements remained in Bordeaux, Avignon, Marseilles, (from where they were evicted in 1682) and in the northern province of Alsace.

SAXONY: Expelled in 1349.

HUNGARY: By 1092 the Jews were in control of Hungary's tax collections. In 1360 they were expelled but later returned. In 1582 they were again expelled from the Christian part of Hungary.

BELGIUM: Expelled in 1370. A few settled there again in 1450, but no large numbers came till 1700.

SLOVAKIA: Ousted from Prague in 1380. Many settled there again after 1562. In 1744 Marie Theresa expelled them again.

AUSTRIA: Expelled in 1420 by Albrecht V.

NETHERLANDS: Expelled from Utrecht in 1444.

SPAIN: Expelled in 1492.

LITHUANIA: Expelled in 1495 by Grand Duke Alexander. They later returned.

PORTUGAL: Expelled in 1498.

PRUSSIA: Expelled in 1510.

ITALY: Expelled from Kingdom of Naples and Sardinia in 1540.

BAVARIA: Banned permanently in 1551.

Jews were not permitted to enter Sweden until 1782. None were permitted to enter Denmark before the 17th century and they were not allowed in Norway after 1814. Today only a handful reside in all Scandinavia.

Back to Poland

By 1500 all of Western Europe except northern Italy, parts of Germany, and the Papal possessions around Avignon, had been rid of the Jewish invasion. For a while, at least, Europe was free of the Jews; not until 1650 did they return in any numbers. Says Encyclopedia Britannica:[5] "The great mass of the Jewish people were thus to be found once more in the East, in the Polish and Turkish empires... The few communities suffered to remain in western Europe were meanwhile subjected at last to all the restrictions which earlier ages had usually allowed to remain as an ideal; so that in a sense, the Jewish dark ages may be said to begin with the Renaissance."

---
5 Encyclopedia Britannica, page 57-58, vol. 13—1947

THE RENAISSANCE
As the Jew Departed...

The period marked by the evictions—1300 to 1650—also marks the period of the Renaissance which broke over Europe as the Jews departed. Starting at first in the trading cities of northern Italy in about 1300, there began a great rebirth of culture and learning which at first was based almost entirely on the writings of the ancient Greeks and Romans. Very quickly this renascent culture spread over Europe and when the age had ended, in about 1650, Europe was by comparison with her former status, enlightened and civilized. Quite obviously all this could not have taken place had it not been for a great upsurge of commercial activity which occurred simultaneously with, and as an adjunct of, the Renaissance. Not until the nations of Europe had wrested commercial control from the ghetto did this rebirth of western civilization occur.

The Ghettos

"Wherever Jews have settled, since the beginning of the Diaspora, they have proceeded to create their own communal organizations. Various factors of an internal character—religious, cultural, social, and economic—as well as external factors, have contributed to this factor" (Page 201, The Jewish People, Past and Present, by the Central Yiddish Culture Organization (CYCO), New York).

It is virtually impossible to comprehend the character of Judaism without some knowledge of the nature of the Medieval Jewish community. (Kahal; Ghetto). Probably one of the commonest fallacies extant today concerns the true origin of the ghetto. Most history books defer to Jewish sensibilities by giving the Jewish version, namely that the Jewish people were for centuries forced to reside in a special quarter of the city as a result of the bigotry and intolerance of the Christian majority. This is not true, and no scholar of Judaism believes it to be.

Valentine's Jewish Encyclopedia describes the origin of the ghetto as follows:

"The word became general for a Jew's quarter. Already in antiquity the Jews voluntarily occupied special quarters; In the Middle Ages, Jew's streets or Jewries were to be found from the end of the 11th century, but the motive of their concentration was no longer religious or social: trade caused them to settle near the market, or danger made them seek the protection of the reigning prince, the protector also wishing to have them together for the easier collection of taxes. It was not until the 13th century that the Jew's quarter was turned into a compulsory Ghetto.... The concentration of Jews in Ghettos, although unintended, had its good result. It preserved the communal feeling and the traditional Jewish culture."

As a point of fact these ghetto-communities existed only because the Jews wanted them to exist—they represented a desire on the part of Jewry to remain aloof and exclusive of Christian Society. Says Valentine's Jewish Encyclopedia:[6] **"There were as a rule officially recognized authorities in the Jewish communities in Europe during the Middle Ages to regulate their own affairs and to treat as a body with the civil government. Even with no other incentive but that of living up to the requirements of**

The Altneuschule, Prague, from the West.

The medieval Jewish ruin dates from the 11th century. In the ghettos the Jews evolved their own language (Yiddish), and preserved a separate nationality.

---

6 Valentine's Jewish Encyclopedia, page 589, Shapiro Valentine Co., London

North Gate of the Jewry at Carpentras. (From the "Revue des Etudes Juives.")

In France, as in other countries, the Jews established their parasitic ghetto-communities. The one in Carpentras dates from the middle ages.

Judaism the Jews of a locality were compelled to organize themselves into a community (Kahal; Kehilla), in order to regulate ritual, educational and charitable institutions. Courts of law were also a necessity, since Jewish litigants were expected to obey the civil code of the Talmud."

The ghetto was not merely a place of residence; it was in the fullest sense a community within a community. Here the Jews maintained their culture, their religion, and their tradition of solidarity. Here they nursed their age-long hatred for Christian civilization. Says Encyclopedia Britannica:[7] **"All these activities necessitated a great deal of legislation and in this the autonomous Jewish community was granted the widest latitude. Ordinances were enacted by Jews governing every phase of life: business, synagogue attendance, social morals, policing, prescriptions for dress, and a detailed regimentation of amusements... The characteristic common to the medieval Jewish community were: self imposed discipline, the** considering of all religious, philanthropic,

[7] Encyclopedia Britannica, p 59, vol. 13—1947.]

educational, and self defense problems as common concerns, and a strong sense of solidarity fortified by a uniform way of life."

For ten centuries preceding the great evictions, in virtually every Christian nation of Europe (and in Mohammedan Spain, Africa, and Asia Minor) these Jews settled into these parasitic ghetto-communities and here they nurtured and maintained a culture which was quite a thing apart from the culture of the European. When finally they were driven from Western Europe in the centuries preceding the Renaissance, we find them settling and establishing ghetto-communities in Poland and Russia which have lasted down to the present day. The Medieval ghetto did not disappear with the ending of the Dark Ages—it was transferred, unimpaired, to Eastern Europe, where the majority of the world's Jews settled.

The institution of the ghetto has enabled two basically different cultures and peoples to remain side by side—one Asiatic and Judaic, the other European and Christian—without becoming integrated. It is primarily for this reason that the Jew has remained an alien in spite of centuries of exposure to Christian civilization. And that is why the Spanish Jew remained a Jew first and a Spaniard second, and why the Polish Jew, the Russian Jew, and the German Jew, have given their first allegiance to Judah and rendered a sort of second-hand loyalty to the country of their abode.

The Chazars

The modern Jew with his Yiddish culture and rapacious financial traditions should not be confused with the biblical Hebrews, who were mainly a pastoral people. The international Jew of modern times is indeed the bastardized product of a bastardized past. He does not truly worship the Bible, but the Talmud; he does not speak Hebrew, but Yiddish; he is not descended from Israel, but from the scum of the eastern Mediterranean. This is vividly illustrated by H. G. Wells in his great Outline of History[8]:

"The Jewish idea was and is a curious combination of theological breadth and an intense racial patriotism. The Jews looked for a special saviour, a Messiah, who was to redeem mankind by the agreeable process of

---
[8] "Outline of History," page 493-494, third edition, by H.G. Wells

Typical late 19th century Jewish family of Cracow (Poland). Believing themselves to be of the "chosen race," they dream of the day when they will "inherit the earth." More than three million of these Polish-Russian Jews have immigrated to the U.S. Most American Jews are of eastern European origin.

restoring the fabulous glories of David and Solomon, and bringing the whole world at last under the benevolent but firm Jewish heel. As the political power of the peoples declined as Carthage followed Tyre into the darkness and Spain became a Roman province, this dream grew and spread. There can be little doubt that the scattered Phoenicians in Spain and Africa and throughout the Mediterranean, speaking as they did a language closely akin to Hebrew and being deprived of their authentic political rights, became proselytes to Judaism. For phases of vigorous proselytism alternated with phases of exclusive jealousy in Jewish history. On one occasion the Idumeans, being conquered, were all forcibly made Jews. (Josephus). There were Arab tribes who were Jews in the time of Muhammad, and a Turkish people who were mainly Jews in South Russia in the ninth century. Judaism is indeed the reconstructed political ideal of many shattered peoples—mainly Semitic. It is to the Phoenician contingent and to Aramean accessions in Babylon that the financial and commercial tradition of the Jews is to be ascribed. But as a result of these coalescences and assimilations, almost everywhere in the towns throughout the Roman Empire, and far beyond it in the east, Jewish communities traded and flourished, and were kept in touch through the Bible, and through a religious and educational organization. The main part of Jewry never was in Judea and had never come out of Judea." [Outline of

History page 493-494, third edition, by H. G. Wells. Section 'Christianity and Islam,' with a footnote recommending the Cambridge Medieval History.]

The "Turkish" people whom Wells mentions were the Chazars [Chazar=Khazar], who built an empire in south Russia in the 9th century A. D. This Chazar empire was infiltrated by large numbers of Byzantine Jews. By process of intermarriage and conversion these Chazars became identified as Jews and in all Jewish histories and encyclopedias the words "Chazar" and "Jew" are used interchangeably. In the tenth century a succession of invasions destroyed the Chazar empire and large numbers of these Chazar-Jews settled in the area of what is now Poland. Others found their way to western Europe and Spain, where they mingled with the already bastardized conglomeration of European Jewry.

This map is based on Britton's reproduction from Funk & Wagnall, itself based on Atlas de Géographie Historique by Schrader. Shading showed Roman Catholics, Greek Catholics,

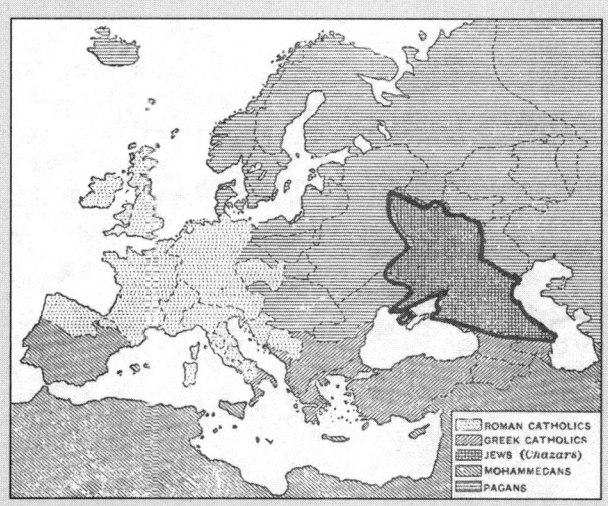

Map showing the Distribution of Religions in Europe in the Tenth Century, indicating Extent of the Kingdom of the Chazars. (After Schrader, "Atlas de Geographie Historique.")

The above map, taken from Funk & Wagnall's Jewish Encyclopedia, shows the extent of the Chazar Empire in the 10th century. The modern Jew is descended from a mixture of Asiatic people, largely Semitic in origin, but no Hebraic.

Mohammedans, Jews, and Pagans.

I've indicated the boundaries, on the same map, of the Khazars, the Pale, and Russia; and emphasized where Ukraine is. The rectangle corresponds to the maps of Poland]

Poland's Fate

These Jews we find settling in Poland in the early 14th century came there at the invitation of Casimir I, who seems to have been under strong Jewish influence. As early as the 10th century the Jews (chiefly of Khazar origin) were influential in Poland, and by the 12th century they were well enough entrenched to monopolize the coinage of Poland's money. Says the Jewish Encyclopedia[9]: "Coins unearthed in 1812 in the Great Polish village of Glenbok show conclusively that in the reigns of Mieczyslauw III (1173-1209), Casimir, and Leshek (1194-1205), the Jews were, as stated above, in charge of the coinage of Great and Little Poland." It is interesting to note that these coins bore Jewish as well as Polish inscriptions.

The history of Poland for the next 3 centuries revolves around the struggle for supremacy between the native Polish people and the Jews. During the greater part of that time Poland was more or less dominated by the Jews—a situation most beneficial to all, according to Jewish history books. But when, as occasionally happened, there was a lapse in Jewish fortunes, these same histories are replete with accounts of gentile cruelty and bestiality to the chosen race. And because these laments have been repeated often enough and loudly enough there is a widely held belief that Poland has been a land of oppression for Jewry...

Polish coins bearing Jewish inscriptions. Jews controlled Europe's money supply during the Dark Ages.

---

9 Funk & Wagnall's Jewish Encyclopedia, page 56, vol. 10

It has been the unhappy fate of Poland to be saddled for the greater part of its history with a large proportion of the world's Jewish population. This, more than anything else, accounts for the tragic disunity which has kept Poland from taking its place among the great nations of the earth.

In 1793 (third partition) Poland was divided between Prussia and Russia and thus ceased to exist as a nation. Russia thus fell heir to a full fledged Jewish problem.

Russia

The third partition of Poland was an event of paramount significance in Russian history because as a by-product of the partition she acquired the world's largest Jewish population. From this moment on Russia's history became hopelessly intertwined with the Jewish problem, and eventually, as we shall relate, the Jews brought about the downfall of Imperial Russia.

No one can possibly understand the nature of present day communism, nor of Zionism, without some knowledge of the situation existing in Russia in the century preceding the October revolution of 1917. We have already noted the presence of Khazar Jews in Poland in the 10th century, and these same Khazar Jews are to be found in Russia from that time on. But whereas Poland had invited the evicted Jews of western Europe to settle in vast numbers within its boundaries in the 13th, 14th, and 15th centuries, the Imperial Russian government had permitted no such immigrations, and had in fact sealed its borders to them. As would be expected, therefore, the Imperial government was something less than enthusiastic over this sudden acquisition of Poland's teeming masses of Jews.

Pale of Settlement

From the very beginning the Tsarist government imposed a set of restrictions designed to protect Russia's economy and culture from the inroads of the Jew. It was decreed (in 1772) that Jews could settle in Greater Russia, but only in certain areas. Within this "Pale of Settlement" Jews were more or less free to conduct their affairs as they pleased. But travel

The Pale of Settlement extended from the Crimea to the Baltic Sea, encompassing an area half as great as western Europe. By 1917, seven million Jews resided there, comprising perhaps half the world's total Jewish population. It was within the Pale of Settlement that the twin philosophies of Communism and Zionism flourished. Both movements grew out of Jewish hatred of Christian civilization (persecutor of the "chosen race"), and both movements have spread wherever Jews have emigrated. The Pale of Settlement has been the reservoir from which the world-wide forces of communism have flowed.

It is worth noting that half of the world's Jewish population now resides in the U.S., and that all but a handful of these are from the Pale, or are descendents of emigrants from the Pale.

or residence beyond the Pale was rigidly restricted, so that in 1897 (date of Russia's 1st census) 93.9% of Russia's Jewish population lived within its boundaries, and only 6% of the total resided in other parts of the Empire. To prevent smuggling, no Jew was permitted to reside within 50 versts of the border.

From the standpoint of Jewish history, the Pale of Settlement ranks as one of the most significant factors of modern times. Here within a single and contiguous area the greater part of Jewry had gathered, and was to remain, for something like 125 years. For the first time Jewry was subjected to a common environment and a common ground of experience. Out of this common experience and environment there evolved the Yiddish speaking Jew of the 20th century. Here too were born the great movements of Zionism and Communism.

The Kahal

We have already remarked upon the habit of Jewry from ancient times of establishing and maintaining their own tribal community (kahal) within the framework of Christian society. We have noted also that as the Jew was driven from Western Europe, he brought with him to Poland this ancient custom. The Kahal was an established institution in Poland, and as the Jews settled within the Pale they set up these autonomous communities here too.

At first the Imperial government recognized the autonomous Kahal organization permitting them to raise taxes and set up courts of law, where only Jewish litigants were concerned.

In addition to the individual communities, there were district Kahal organizations which at first were permitted to assess local Jewish communities with taxes. In 1786 these privileges were drastically curtailed and Jews were there after obliged to appear before ordinary courts of law and the Kahal organization was restricted to matters of religious and social nature.

Although Jewish propagandists have complained long and loudly of being oppressed by the Imperial government, it is a fact that up until 1881 they prospered beyond all expectation. Jewry settled in the Russian economy like a swarm of locusts

Tsar Alexander I

in a field of new corn. Very quickly they achieved a monopoly over Russia's liquor, tobacco, and retail industries. Later they dominated the professions as well. Under the reign of Alexander I many of the restrictions against residence beyond the Pale of Settlement were relaxed, especially for the artisan and professional classes. A determined effort was made to establish Jews in agriculture and the government encouraged at every opportunity the assimilation of Jews into Russian national life.

Nicholas I

Alexander's successor, Nicholas I, was less inclined to favor Jewry, and in fact viewed their inroads into the Russian economy with alarm. He was much hated by the Jews. Prior to his reign, Alexander I had allowed any male Jew the privilege of escaping compulsory military duty by paying a special draft-exemption tax. In 1827 Nicholas abolished the custom, with the result that Jews were for the first time taken into the Imperial armies...

In 1844 Nicholas I further antagonized Jewry by abolishing the institution of the Kahal, and in that same year he prohibited by law the traditional Jewish garb,

Tsar Nicholas I

specifying that all Jews should, except on ceremonial occasions, dress in conformity with Russian standards. These measures, and many others like them, were aimed at facilitating the assimilation of Jewry into Russian life. The Tsarist government was much concerned by the Jew's failure to become Russianized, and viewed with extreme hostility the ancient Jewish custom of maintaining a separate culture, language, mode of dress, etc.—all of which contributed to keep the Jew an alien in the land of his residence. It is to this determination to "Russianize" and "civilize" the Jew that we can ascribe the unusual efforts made by the Imperial government to provide free education to its Jews. In 1804 all schools were thrown open to Jews and attendance for Jewish children was made compulsory. Compulsory education was not only a novelty in Russia, but in any country in the early 19th century. In Russia education was generally reserved for a privileged few, and even as late as 1914 only 55% of her gentile population had been inside a school. The net result of the Imperial government's assimilation program was that Russian Jewry became the best educated segment in Russia. This eventually worked to the destruction of the Tsarist government...

Typical male attire of a late 19th century Jew. A different mode of dress, a different language, and a different culture helped him retain his Jewishness.

The reign of Alexander II marked the apex of Jewish fortunes in Tsarist Russia. By 1880 they were becoming dominant in the professions, in many trades and industries, and were beginning to filter into government in increasing numbers. As early as 1861 Alexander II had permitted Jewish university graduates to settle and hold governmental positions in greater Russia, and by 1879 apothecaries, nurses, midwives dentists, distillers, and skilled craftsmen were permitted to work and reside throughout the empire.

Nevertheless Russia's Jews were increasingly rebellious over the remaining restraints which still bound the greater part of Russian Jewry to the Pale of Settlement, and which, to some extent at least, restricted their commercial activities. Herein lay the dilemma; the Imperial government could retain certain of the restrictions against the Jews, and by doing so incur their undying hostility, or it could remove all restraints and thus pave the way for Jewish domination over every phase of Russian life. Certainly Alexander viewed this problem with increasing concern as time went on. Actually it was a problem capable of being solved.

Tsar Alexander II

Alexander II lost a considerable amount of his enthusiasm for liberal causes after an attempt was made to assassinate him in 1866. He dismissed his "liberal" advisors and from that time on displayed an inclination toward conservatism. This is not to say he became anti-Jewish, but he did show more firmness in dealing with them. In 1879 there was another attempt on his life, and another in the following year when his winter palace was blown up. In 1881 a plot hatched in the home of the Jewess, Hesia Helfman, was successful. Alexander II was blown up and so ended an era.

The New Policy

The reaction to the assassination of Alexander II was instantaneous and far reaching. There was a widespread belief in and out of the government, that if the Jews were dissatisfied with the rule of Alexander II—whom the crypto-Jew, D'Israeli, had described as "the most benevolent prince that ever ruled Russia"—then they would be satisfied with nothing less than outright domination of Russia.

Up to 1881 Russian policy had consistently been directed in an attempt to "Russianize" the Jew, preparatory to accepting him into full citizenship. In line with this policy, free and compulsory education for Jews had been introduced, repeated attempts had been made to encourage them to settle on farms, and special efforts had been made to encourage them to engage in the crafts. Now Russian policy was reversed. Hereafter it became the policy of the Imperial government to prevent the further exploitation of the Russian people by the Jews. Thus began the death struggle between Tsar and Jew.

All through 1881 there was widespread anti-Jewish rioting all over the empire. Large numbers of Jews who had been permitted to settle beyond the Pale of Settlement were evicted. In May of 1882 the May Laws (Provisional Rules of May 3, 1882) were imposed, thus implementing the new governmental policy.

The May Laws shook the empire to its foundations. The following passage is taken from Encyclopedia Britannica[10]: **"The Russian May Laws were the most conspicuous legislative monument achieved by modern anti-Semitism... Their immediate results was a ruinous commercial depression which was felt all over the empire and which profoundly affected the national credit. The Russian minister was at his wit's end for money. Negotiations for a large loan were entered upon with the house of Rothschild and a preliminary contract was signed, when... the finance minister was informed that unless the persecutions of the Jews were stopped the great banking house would be compelled to withdraw from the operation... In this way anti-Semitism, which had already so profoundly influenced the domestic policies of Europe, set its mark on the international relations of the powers, for it was the urgent need of the Russian treasury quite as much as the termination of Prince Bismarck's secret treaty of mutual neutrality which brought about the Franco-Russian alliance."**

Thus, within a period of 92 years (from the 3rd partition to 1882) the Jews, although constituting only 4.2% of the

---
10 Encyclopedia Britannica [page 76, volume 2, 1947]

population, had been able to entrench themselves so well in the Russian economy that the nation was almost bankrupted in the attempt to dislodge them. And, as we have seen, the nation's international credit was also affected.

After 1881 events served increasingly to sharpen the enmity of Jewry toward Tsarism. The May Laws had not only restricted Jewish economic activity, but had attempted—unsuccessfully, as we shall see—to preserve Russia's cultural integrity. Hereafter Jews were permitted to attend state-supported schools and universities, but only in ratio to their population. This was not unreasonable since Russia's schools were flooded with Jewish students while large numbers of her gentile population were illiterate, but to the Jews this represented another bitter "persecution," and all the world was acquainted with the enormity of this new crime against Jewry...

On May 23rd a delegation of Jews headed by Baron Gunzberg called on the new Tsar (Alexander III) to protest the May Laws and the alleged discrimination against Jewry. As a result of the investigation which followed, Tsar Alexander issued an edict the following Sept. 3rd, a part of which is given here:

"**For some time the government has given its attention to the Jews and to their relations to the rest of the inhabitants of the empire, with a view of ascertaining the sad condition of the Christian inhabitants brought about by the conduct of the Jews in business matters...**

Tsar Alexander III

During the last twenty years the Jews have gradually possessed themselves of not only every trade and business in all its branches, but also of a great part of the land by buying or farming it. With few exceptions, they have as a body devoted their attention, not

to enriching or benefiting the country, but to defrauding by their wiles its inhabitants, and particularly its poor inhabitants. This conduct of theirs has called forth protests on the part of the people, as manifested in acts of violence and robbery. The government, while on the one hand doing its best to put down the disturbances, and to deliver the Jews from oppression and slaughter, have also, on the other hand, thought it a matter of urgency and justice to adopt stringent measures in order to put an end to the oppression practised by the Jews on the inhabitants, and to free the country from their malpractices, which were, as is known, the cause of the agitations."[11]

It was in this atmosphere that the twin movements of Marxism and Zionism began to take hold and dominate the mass of Russian Jewry. Ironically, both Zionism and Marxism were first promulgated by westernized German Jews. Zionism, whose chief advocate was Theodore Herzl, took root in Russia in the 1880s in competition with Marxism, whose high priest was Karl Marx, grandson of a rabbi... Eventually every Russian Jew came to identify himself with either one or the other of these movements.

THE TERROR SECTION

Six Assassinated

As an outgrowth of this political fermentation, there appeared at the beginning of the century one of the most remarkable terroristic organizations ever recorded in the annals of history. This was the Jewish dominated **Social Revolutionary Party**, which between 1901 and 1906 was responsible for the assassination of no less than six first ranking leaders of the Imperial government, including Minister of Education Bogolepov (1901); Minister of Interior Sipyagin (1902); Governor of Ufa Bogdanovich (1903); Premier Viachelav von Plehve (1904); Grand Duke Sergei, uncle of the Tsar (1905); and General Dubrassov, who had suppressed the Moscow insurrection (1906).

Chief architect of these terroristic activities was the Jew,

---

[11] Russia and Turkey in the 19th Century by E. W. Latimer, page 332. A. C. McClury & Co., 1895.

The Jew, Gershuni, masterminded the Terror against the Tsar's ministers. Meanwhile, Jews the world over spread hate propaganda against the Imperial government.

Gershuni, who headed the "terror section" of the **Social Revolutionary Party**. In charge of the "fighting section" was Yevno Azev, son of a Jewish tailor, and one of the principal founders of the party.

Azev later plotted, but was unable to carry out, the assassination of Tsar Nicholas II. He was executed in 1909 and Gershuni was sentenced to life imprisonment. This marked the end of the terroristic activities of the party, but the effect of these political murders was far reaching. Never again was the royal family, or its ministers, free from the fear of assassination. Soon another prime minister would be shot down—this time in the very presence of the Tsar. This was the backdrop for the revolution of 1905.

BLOODY SUNDAY

The revolution of 1905, like that of 1917, occurred in an atmosphere of war. On Jan. 2nd, 1905, the Japanese captured Port Arthur, and thereby won the decisive victory of the [Russo-Japanese] war. Later in January there occurred a tragic incident which was the immediate cause of the 1905 revolution, and which was to affect the attitude of Russia's industrial population toward the Tsar for all time. This was the "Bloody Sunday" affair.

The Imperial government, in its attempts to gain the favor of the industrial population, and in its search for a way to combat Jewish revolutionary activity, had adopted the tactic of encouraging the formation of legal trade unions, to which professional agitators were denied membership. These trade unions received official recognition and were protected by law.

Father Gapon

One of the most outstanding trade union leaders—and certainly the most unusual—was Father Gapon, a priest in the Russian Orthodox Church. On the day Port Arthur fell a number of clashes occurred in Petersberg's giant Putilov works between members of Father Gapon's labor organization and company officials. A few days later the Putilov workers went on strike.

Father Gapon resolved to take the matter directly to the Tsar. On the following Sunday thousands of Petersberg's workmen and their families turned out to participate in this appeal to the "little father." The procession was entirely orderly and peaceful and the petitioners carried patriotic banners expressing loyalty to the crown. At the palace gate the procession was met by a flaming volley of rifle fire. Hundreds of workmen and members of their families were slaughtered. This was "Bloody Sunday," certainly one of the blackest days in Tsarist history.

Was Tsar Nicholas II responsible for Bloody Sunday, as Marxist propagandists have claimed? He couldn't have been because he was out of the city at the time. Father Gapon had marched on an empty palace. But the harm had been done.

Bloody Sunday turned Russia's industrial population against the Tsar. Jew agitators capitalized on this to promote the 1905 revolution. Chief leader of the 1905 revolt was Trotsky.

Revolution of 1905

Bloody Sunday marked the beginning of the 1905 revolution. For the first time the Jewish-Marxists were joined by large numbers of the working class. Bloody Sunday delivered Russia's industrial population into the hands of the Jew-dominated revolutionary movement.

A strike broke out in Lodz in late January, and by June 22nd this developed into an armed insurrection in which 2000 were killed. The Tsar acted at once to recover the situation. In early February he ordered an investigation (by the Shidlovsky Commission) into the causes of unrest among the Petersberg workers, and later in the year (August) he announced provisions for establishing a legislature which later came to be the Duma. Not only that but he offered amnesty to political offenders, under which, incidentally, Lenin returned to Russia. But these attempts failed.

On October 20th the Jewish Menshevik-led All-Russian Railway union went on strike. On the 21st a general strike was called in Petersberg, and on the 25th there were general strikes in Moscow, Smolensk, Kursk, and other cities.

PETERSBERG SOVIET

Trotzky in Power

On October 26th the revolutionary Petersberg Soviet was founded. This Petersberg Soviet assumed the functions of a national government. It issued decrees, proclaimed an eight hour day, freedom of the press, and otherwise exercised the prerogatives of a government.

President of the 1905 Petersberg Soviet was Trotzky. In 1917 he was president of the second Petersberg Soviet during the Bolshevik Revolution.

From the very beginning the Soviet was dominated by the Menshevik faction of the **Russian Social-Democratic Labor Party**, although the **Social Revolutionary Party** was also represented. Its first president was the Menshevik, Zborovski, who was succeeded by Georgii Nosar. He in turn was succeeded by Lev Trotzky, who chiefly as a result of the prestige gained in 1905, became one of the guiding spirits of the October revolution in 1917.

Trotzky became president of the Petersberg Soviet on Dec. 9th, and a week later some 300 members of the Soviet, including Trotzky, were arrested. The revolution was almost, but not quite over.

Parvus

On Dec. 20th the Jew, Parvus, assumed control of a new executive committee of the Soviet and organized a general strike in Petersberg which involved 90,000 workers. The next day 150,000 workers went on strike in Moscow, and there were insurrections in Chita, Kansk, and Rostov. But within a week the government had gained the upper hand and by the 30th of December the revolution was over.

After 1905

As an outcome of the 1905 revolution, Tsar Nicholas II set about remedying the shortcomings of his regime in a most commendable manner. At his decree, Russia was given representative government and a constitution. An elective legislative—the Duma—was established, and free elections were held. By these measures and others which followed, Russia seemed well on the way to becoming a constitutional monarchy patterned after the western European model, and as a point of fact it was only the outbreak of World War I which prevented this from becoming a reality.

As would be expected,

Nicholas II, last of the Tsars.

the Jewish revolutionary parties bitterly opposed these reforms, looking on them as merely a device by which the forces of revolution would be dissipated. Actually these measures did succeed in pacifying the Russian masses, and the years between 1905 and 1914 were ones of comparative quiet and progress. No man deserves more credit for this state of affairs than Premier Peter Arkadyevich Stolypin, who in the year following the 1905 revolt emerged as the most impressive figure in Imperial Russia.

From 1906 to 1911 it is no exaggeration to say that he dominated Russian politics. It was he who gave Russia the famed "Stolypin Constitution," which among other things undertook to guarantee the civil rights of the peasantry, which constituted 85% of Russia's population. His land reforms, for which he is most famous, not only gave the peasant the right to own land, but actually financed the purchase with government loans. Stolypin was determined to give the peasant a stake in capitalism, believing that "the natural counterweight of the communal principal is individual ownership."

Were the Stolypin land reforms effective? Bertram Wolfe, who is on all points anti-Tsarist and pro-revolutionary, has this to say[12]: **"Between 1907 and 1914, under the Stolypin land reform laws, 2,000,000 peasant families seceded from the village mir and became individual proprietors. All through the war the movement continued, so that by Jan. 1, 1916, 6,200,000 peasant families, out of approximately 16,000,000 eligible, had made application for separation. Lenin saw the matter as a race with time between Stolypin's reforms and the next upheaval. Should an upheaval be postponed for a couple of decades, the new land measures would so transform the countryside that it would no longer be a revolutionary force. How near Lenin came to losing the race is proved by the fact that in 1917, when he called on the peasants to "take the land," they already owned more than three-fourths of it."**

Russian Jewry wanted revolution, not reform. As early as 1906 an attempt had been made to assassinate Premier Stolypin when his country house was destroyed by a bomb.

---
12 Three Who Made a Revolution, page 360, by Bertram Wolfe, Dial Press, New York, 1948

Finally in Sept. of 1911 the best premier Russia ever had was shot down in cold blood while attending a gala affair at the Kiev theatre. The assassin was a Jewish lawyer named Mordecai Bogrov. Thus it was that Russia had since 1902 lost two premiers to Jewish assassins.

Many of Stolypin's reforms were carried out after his death. In 1912 an industrial insurance law was inaugurated which gave all industrial workmen sickness and accident compensation to the extent of two-thirds and three-fourths of their regular pay. For the first time the newspapers of the revolutionary parties were given legal status. Public schools were expanded and the election laws were revised. In 1913 a general amnesty for all political prisoners was given. Not even the severest critic of Tsarism can deny that these measures represented a sincere attempt on the part of the Imperial government to bring about reform. Why in spite of all this, was the Tsar overthrown?

Premier Stolypin was shot by a Jew assassin after bringing reform to Russia.

World War I

One of the chief factors contributing to the destruction of the Imperial government was the onset of World War I. Before the war the Imperial military establishment had contained perhaps 1,500,000 professional troops, well trained and loyal to the crown,...[13] **"but by 1917 the regular army was gone. Its losses for the first ten months of the war were reckoned as 3,800,000, or, to take the reckoning of the Quartermaster-General, Danilov, 300,000 a month and the officers, who went into action standing, while commanding their men to crawl, were falling at**

---
[13] Russia, page 41, by Bernard Pares, New American Library, New York, revised 1949.

These Cossack troops were the elite of the Tsar's regular army.

twice the rate of the men." Altogether 18 million men were called to the colors, most of whom were conscripted from the peasantry. Although courageous in battle they proved politically unreliable and were easily incited by agitators.

Large numbers of the industrial population were also drafted into the armies, and their places were taken by peasants, fresh out of the country. As a result, Russia's principal cities came to be populated by a working class which was peasant in origin and habit of thinking, but which lacked the conservatism and stability which seems to go with tenure of the land. This new proletariat was in reality an uprooted and landless peasantry, poorly adjusted to city life, and easily stirred up by propagandists.

Now—It should be remembered that the Russian revolution was carried out by a handful of revolutionaries operating mainly in the larger cities. While something like 85% of Russia's gentile population was rural, these country people took virtually no part in the revolt. Conversely only 2.4% of the Jewish population was actually situated on the farms; the great majority of the Jews were congregated in the cities. Says the Universal Jewish Encyclopedia[14]: "...it must be noted that the Jews lived almost exclusively in the cities and

---
[14] page 285, vol. 9, Universal Jewish Encyclopedia, Inc., New York, 1939

towns; in Russia's urban population the Jews constituted 11%. Two additional factors are taken into consideration. On the one hand the rural population took practically no part in political activities, and on the other there was virtually no illiteracy among the Russian Jews." As a matter of fact, the Jews represented a substantial portion of Russia's educated class. Not only that, but the overwhelming majority of Russia's professional class were Jews. So complete was the Jewish domination of the professions that only one out of eight of Russia's professional people were gentile. In other words, the Jews, who constituted 4.2% of Russia's pre-war population comprised something like 87% of its professional class.

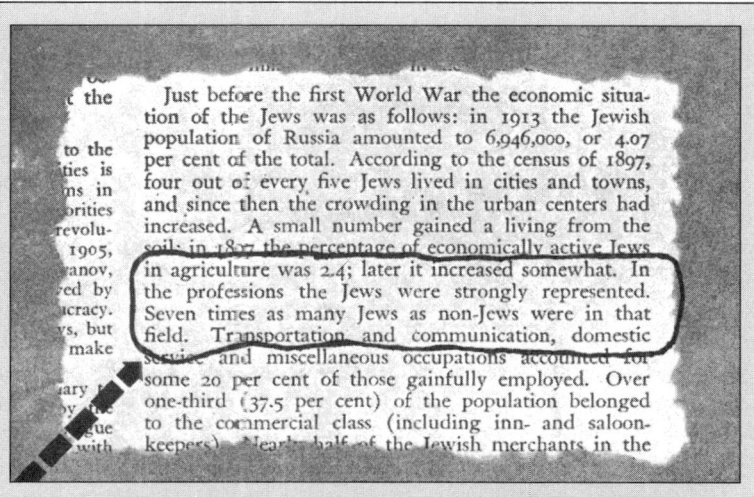

The above excerpt is taken from the Universal Jewish Encyclopedia (p. 228, vol. 9). It shows that seven-eighths of Russia's pre-war professional class were Jews. It also shows that the majority of Jews were congregated in the cities, and that 37% of them belonged to the "commercial class." This explains better than anything else why Jewry was able to dominate Russia's urban centers. In 1913 only 15% of Russia's gentile population lived in the cities, and many of these were freshly recruited from an illiterate peasantry.

The Evacuations

Also significant was the fact that the theatre of war was situated in those areas most heavily populated by Jews. By 1914, it should be remembered, Russia's Jewish population was nearing the seven million mark. (The exact figure given in the Universal Jewish Encyclopedia is 6,946,000). A substantial number of these resided in Russian-Poland, which was a war zone. The majority of these Jews, out of hatred for the Tsarist regime, were inclined to favor a German victory. As a result, the Imperial high command was compelled to remove all Jews from the war area in the early part of 1915. In May of 1915, for example, the supreme command expelled all Jewish residents from the provinces of Courland and Grodno. Altogether, nearly a half million Jews were forced to leave their homes in the military zone. These expellees were at first required to remain within the Pale of Settlement, but in August of 1915 they were permitted to settle in all cities in the empire. Thus it was that as the war progressed a flood of Tsar-hating Jews began infiltrating the cities beyond the Pale...

REVOLUTION

The revolution occurred in March of 1917, in St. Petersberg, capital city of the Romanovs. From beginning to end the revolt involved an amazingly small number of people when we consider that the fate of 150 million Russians was at stake. The revolt came, as we have tried to indicate, because of Jewish unrest, because of Jewry's dissatisfaction, and above all, because of Jewry's determination to destroy Tsarism. By the Spring of 1917 Russia's unstable urban population had been thoroughly poisoned by this dissatisfaction. A food shortage in Petersberg fanned this dissatisfaction into the flame of revolution.

St. Petersberg in the third year of World War I was Russia's chief armaments production center, and by reason of this possessed the largest industrial population of any city in Russia. It also had the largest Jewish population of any city outside the Pale of Settlement. By March, 1917, a breakdown in the Russian transportation system resulted in a severe food shortage in the city. At the same time, many of the city's factories began shutting down due to material shortages. Both of these factors were extremely important in the days immediately ahead.

The desperate food shortage affected virtually every family in the city. Furthermore, the enforced idleness of the working population—due to factory shutdowns—threw vast numbers of workmen onto the streets. Given here is a day by day account of the events which resulted in the overthrow of the Tsar and the establishment of the Provisional Government:

March 5th: It was evident by this time—even to foreign visitors—that trouble was brewing. Bread lines were growing day by day, and factory workmen began to appear on the streets in large numbers. During the day the police began mounting machine guns in strategic places throughout the city.

March 6th: The government brought a large number of Cossack troops into the city in anticipation of trouble. Revolution was now freely predicted, and many of the shops in expectation of this began boarding up windows. The few remaining factories were closed by strikes and the police mounted more machine guns. The Tsar, who was visiting the troops at the front, still had not returned to the city. The Duma remained in session.

A breakdown in the Russian transportation system resulted in a bread shortage in St. Petersberg. This picture shows women queuing up before a bakery a few days before the Revolution.

March 8th: Crowds of women began a series of street demonstrations in protest over the bread shortage. Agitators, many of whom were veterans of the 1905 revolution, began to take charge and organize diversionary demonstrations.

Here and there the crowds sang the "Marseillaise"—regarded in Russia as a revolutionary song. A number of red flags appeared. At the corner of Nevsky Prospekt and the Catherine Canal mounted police, aided by Cossack cavalry, dispersed the crowds. There were no casualties. Significantly, however, the crowds had raised the red flag of revolution without being fired on.

March 9th: The Nevsky from Catherine Canal to Nicolai Station was jammed from early morning with crowds, which were larger and bolder than on the preceding day. Streetcars were no longer running. The Cossack cavalry, under orders to keep the Nevsky clear of demonstrators, repeatedly charged the mobs, and a few people were trampled. But it was observed that the cavalrymen used only the flats of their sabres, and at no time used fire arms. This encouraged the

The transportation breakdown caused Petersberg's factories to close down, throwing thousands of workmen onto the streets. Hungry and unemployed, they fell easy prey to red agitators.

mob, which held the Cossacks in dread. Meanwhile, agitators were constantly at work.

March 10th: During the afternoon huge crowds collected around Nicholai Station. An American photographer, Donald Thompson, has described in vivid fashion the scene there[15]:

"**About two o'clock a man richly dressed in furs**

---
15 Donald Thompson in Russia, page 54, by Donald Thompson, Century Co.. New York, 1918

came up to the square in a sleigh and ordered his driver to go through the crowd, which by this time was in a very ugly mood, although it seemed to be inclined to make way for him. He was impatient and probably cold and started an argument. All Russians must have their argument. Well, he misjudged this crowd, and also misjudged the condition in Petrograd. I was within 150 feet of this scene. He was dragged out of his sleigh and beaten. He took refuge in a stalled street car where he was followed by the workingmen. One of them took a small iron bar and beat his head to a pulp. This seemed to give the mob a taste for blood. Immediately I was pushed along in front of the crowd which surged down the Nevsky and began smashing windows and creating general disorder. Many of the men carried red flags on sticks. The shops along the Nevsky, or most of them, are protected by heavy iron shutters. Those that were not had their windows smashed. I noticed about this time that ambulances were coming and going on the side streets. There were usually three or four people lying in each one."

The disorder now became general. The mobs turned their fury on the police, who barricaded themselves for a desperate last stand in the police stations. There they were slaughtered almost to the last man, and the prisons were emptied of their

The Petersberg mob marching under the red flag of revolution. The end was in sight.

On March 10th, 1917, the only thing holding the Petersberg mob in check was the police. The decisive moment of the revolution came when armed mobs stormed the police stations, killing the police and freeing large numbers of convicts, many of whom were the worst type of criminals.

One of the first acts of the mob after storming the police stations was to burn police archives. Later the few policemen allowing themselves to be captured were shot. With the mob in control, life in Petersberg became chaotic. Servants refused to work, shops closed, workmen demanded fantastic wages. It was dangerous for a well dressed man to appear in public.

entire populations, including desperate criminals of every category.

March 11th: Widespread rioting continued on the 11th. Added to the terror of revolution were the degradations of the recently liberated criminal population. During the day the

Duma sent the following urgent message to the Tsar, now entrained for Petersberg: "The situation is serious. There is anarchy in the capital. The government is paralyzed. The situation as regards transportation, and supplies, and fuel has reached a state of complete disorganization. Police dissatisfaction is growing. Disorderly shooting is taking place in the streets. Different sections of the troops are shooting at each other. It is necessary immediately to intrust a person who has the confidence of the country with the creation of a new government."

The Tsar's reaction was tragically out of keeping with the reality of the situation. It is doubtful that he even had an inkling of what was really transpiring. His reaction was to command the dissolution of the Duma. The overwhelming majority of the Duma's membership,—loyal to the Tsar— obeyed his command, with the result that the last vestige of governmental authority ceased to exist in the capital.

March 12th: The president of the dissolved Duma sent this last despairing message to the Tsar: "The situation is becoming worse. Immediate means must be taken, for tomorrow it will be too late. The last hour has struck and the fate of the fatherland and the dynasty is being decided." Tsar Nicholas II may never have received the message: in any event he did not reply. And indeed, the hour was late...

At 1:00 A.M. on the morning of the 12th one of the regiments (the Volynski) revolted, killing its officers. By 11 A.M. six regiments had

Crowds demonstrating before the Duma. On March 12th, twelve members of the Duma formed a "Provisional Government" which was to rule Russia for 8 months.

revolted. At 11:30 A.M. the garrison of the Peter and Paul fortress surrendered and joined the revolution. The only section of the city which now remained under governmental control was the War Office, the Admiralty Building, and St. Isaac's Cathedral. The revolution was now an accomplished fact. Four days later, on the 16th, the Tsar, whose train never reached Petersberg, abdicated. The closing words of his written abdication announcement were: "May God have mercy on Russia." And before a year had passed, these words had been echoed many, many times...

The 12th of March marked the formation of two governing bodies which were to jointly rule Russia for the next 8 months. The first of these was the Provisional Committee of the Duma, consisting of 12 members headed by Prince Lvow. This group served as the Provisional Government until overthrown in October by the Bolsheviks. At all times, however, it governed by the sufferance of the Petersberg Soviet, which was the second body organized on the l2th.

This Petersberg Soviet was in reality dominated by the Menshevik and Bolshevik factions of the Russian Social Democratic Labor Party, of whom the Mensheviks were by far the most powerful. A second party, the Social Revolutionary Party, was a minority party.

Eventually, as we shall see, the Bolshevik faction gained control over the Petersberg Soviet, and having done so, at once precipitated the October Revolution and established the regime which is still in power. To better understand these events, it is necessary that we trace the history of these Mensheviks and Bolsheviks and their Russian Social Democratic Labor Party.

HISTORY OF BOLSHEVISM

We must for the moment turn our attention to a group of revolutionary exiles who are important to this story because they and their disciples eventually became the rulers of Communist Russia. Head of this group, and the man who is generally recognized as Lenin's teacher, was George Plekhanov, a gentile.

Plekhanov had fled Russia in the 1880s and settled in Switzerland. There with the aid of Vera Zasulich, Leo Deutch, and P. Axelrod—all Jews—he had formed the Marxist "Group for the Emancipation of Labor," and until 1901 was recognized as the leader of the group.

Although Plekanov was himself a gentile, those around him were, with a few exceptions, Jewish.

Lenin

Lenin (real name Vladimir Ilyich Ulyanov) was born on the banks of the Volga in the provincial city of Simbirsk, in 1870. He was born to a station of comparative privilege, being the son of a government official whose title of "Actual State Counsellor" carried with it the privilege of hereditary nobility. Lenin's father did not himself inherit the title, but acquired it as a reward of service as a school supervisor.

By every rule, "Lenin" should have become a respected member of Russian society. He was of middle class background, was university educated, and was admitted to the practice of law. That he did not do so can be ascribed in part to the fate of his older brother, Alexander, who in 1887 was executed for participating in an attempt on the life of Tsar Alexander II. This is said to have influenced Lenin to take up the career of a professional revolutionary.

In any event the year of 1895 finds young Lenin—then 25—meeting in Switzerland with the leaders of the "Group for the Emancipation of Labor." Shortly thereafter he returned to Russia in the company of young Julius Martov (Tsederbaum), a Jew who had already

Plekhanov

Lenin a confirmed Jew was married to Krupsakaya. He headed the Lenin-Zinoviev-Kamenev "troika."

become prominent as an agitator in the Pale of Settlement, and who was one day to become the leader of the Menshevik faction. Their purpose was to raise funds for revolutionary activity.

In Petersberg they became involved in a series of strikes which swept the city in 1895, and in the autumn of the same year Lenin, Martov, and a number of others were convicted and sent to prison for revolutionary activity.

In February of 1897 Lenin completed his prison term and began his period of exile in Siberia. He was permitted to travel to Siberia at his own expense and he took with him his Jewish wife, Krupsakaya and her Yiddish speaking mother.

Krupsakaya

It should be explained that, contrary to popular belief, political exiles—unless convicted of a criminal act—were not imprisoned in Siberia; rather they were paroled there. In exile the government provided a pension, sufficient usually to maintain an existence. To supplement this, the exile sometimes sought local employment (Trotzky worked as a bookkeeper) or they got funds from friends and family. Lenin received a government allowance of 7 rubles 40 kopeks monthly, "enough to pay for room, board and laundry."[16]

While in Siberian exile Lenin, Martov, and an accomplice Potresov, formulated the idea of an "All Russian Newspaper" which would serve to combine the thought and energies of the entire revolutionary movement. The Marxists in 1900, as at all times in the future were divided and subdivided into a great many factions. Lenin's idea was to weld these various factions into a single organization.

Iskra

In February of 1900 Lenin was released from exile and applied for, and got, permission to go to Switzerland. In

---

16 Lenin (abridgement by Donald P. Geddes), page 26, by David Shub, New American Library, 1950 (Mentor Books).]

Geneva he joined the "Group for the Emancipation of Labor," and in December the Group began the publication of **Iskra** (The Spark). The establishment of Iskra marked the beginning of Russian Marxism as an organized movement, and the beginning of Lenin's role as a party leader.

The editorial board consisted of the "oldsters," Plekhanov, Zasulich, Axelrod, and their disciples, Lenin, Potresov, and Martov.[17] Lenin's Jewish wife, Krupsakaya, was the board's secretary. Later, in 1902, young Trotzky (Bronstein) joined the editorial board, but without voting privileges. Four of the above—Martov, Axelrod, Zasulich, and Trotzky—were Jews, while Plekhanov, Lenin, and Potresov were gentile. The editorial board thus contained four Jews and three gentiles, but since Trotzky was without vote, and since Plekhanov had retained two votes, the voting strength was exactly reversed, with the Jews having 3 votes to the gentile's four.

It is interesting to note the editorial contributions of the first 45 editions of Iskra. The largest number of articles was written by Martov, who contributed 39. Next was Lenin, who wrote 32 articles, followed by Plekhanov with 24, Petresov with 8, Zasulich with 6, and Axelrod with 4. In addition, articles were written by Parvus, Trotzky, and Rosa Luxemberg, all of whom were Jewish. It is worth recording that the only other revolutionary paper in existence at this time was "Rabochee Delo" (Workers Cause), organ of the "Economist" faction, of whom the Jew, Theodore Dan was the editor.

Iskra was actually printed in Munich, Germany. For a time the editorial board met in London, but in 1903 it was moved back to Geneva. From there copies of Iskra were smuggled into Russia by ship and courier. In this way Iskra built up an underground organization of professional revolutionaries, first known as "Iskrists," and later as Bolsheviks and Mensheviks.

Communism as an organised movement began with the publishing of ISKRA (The Spark) in December of 1900. Three years later, in 1903, the "Iskrists" joined with the Polish Social Democrats, the Jewish Bund, and others, to form the Russian Social-Democratic Labor Party (which later changed

---

17 In Switzerland Axelrod eked out an existence by peddling yogurt, and Plekhanov is said to have addressed letters for an income. But the founders and leaders of communism were not proletarians. Almost without exception they were highly educated Jewish intellectuals, few of whom had ever performed a useful day's labor.

its name to the Communist Party). ISKRA, like every other Communist publication which followed, was mainly edited and controlled by Jews.

Unification Congress

In 1903 a Unification Congress convened in Brussels, Belgium. Its purpose was to unite the various Marxists groups into the Russian Social-Democratic Labor Party, which technically had been formed in 1898, but which had failed to bring unity.

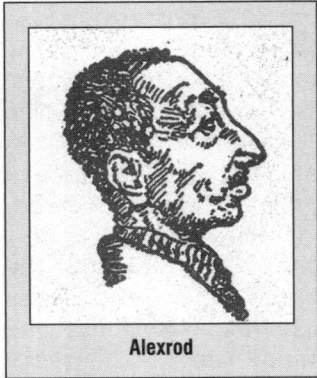
Alexrod

Altogether, 60 voting delegates attended, four of whom were, or had been, workers. The rest were mostly Jewish intellectuals. Represented were the groups which had formed the party in 1898: The Jewish Bund, the Georgian Social Democrats, Rosa Luxemberg's Polish Social democrats, and the Group for the Emancipation of Labor, now identified as "Iskrists." The Maximalist's newspaper, "Rabochee Delo" was also represented by 3 delegates. These groups, their leaders, and their disciples, made the revolution of 1917. Here, Communism as we know it, was born.

In early August the Belgium Police deported a number of delegates and the Unification Congress moved en masse to England, where it convened from August 11th to the 23rd. One very important outcome of the congress was the ideological split which divided the Iskrists into two camps: The Bolsheviks (majority faction), headed by Lenin and the Mensheviks (minority faction), headed by Martov.

The final act of the congress was to elect Lenin, Plekhanov, and Martov to the editorial board of Iskra. This new board of three never actually functioned, due to the hostility between Martov and Lenin. After issue No. 53 Lenin resigned leaving it in the hands of Martov, Plekhanov, Axelrod, Zasulich and Petresov, the latter three being admitted to the board following Lenin's resignation.

Although Lenin's faction clung to the Bolshevik label, they did not at any time command a real majority in the party.

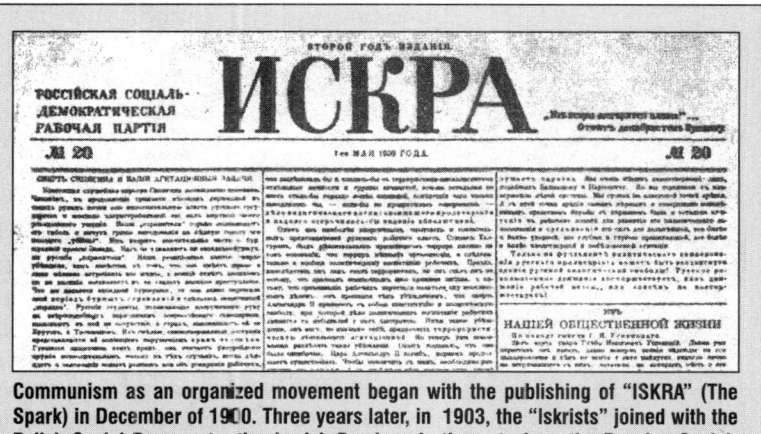

Communism as an organized movement began with the publishing of "ISKRA" (The Spark) in December of 1900. Three years later, in 1903, the "Iskrists" joined with the Polish Social Democrats, the Jewish Bund, and others, to form the Russian Social-Democratic Labor Party (which later changed its name to the Communist Party). "ISKRA," like every other communist publication, which followed, was mainly edited and controlled by Jews.

Lenin had temporarily been able to dominate the Unification Congress when the Jewish Bund's delegation had walked out in a huff over party policy. Because Lenin had been temporarily able to martial a majority of the remaining delegates to his support, his faction had been identified as the Bolshevik, or majority faction, and always thereafter Lenin and his followers were known as Bolsheviks. It is important to note that this Bolshevik-Menshevik split was among the Iskrists only. The two other major factions of the party—Rosa Luxemberg's Polish Social Democrats and the Jewish Bund—were neither Bolshevik nor Menshevik, although both factions usually teamed up with the Mensheviks on party policy. (In 1917, however, both the Polish party and the Bund merged into the Bolshevik faction.)

Revolution of 1905

The 1905 revolution came unexpectedly. Jewish agitators, seizing upon the discontent engendered by Russia's defeat by the Japanese, and capitalizing on the "Bloody Sunday" incident—which we have already described—fanned the flames of insurrection into being in what was to be a dress rehearsal of the 1917 revolution.

The revolt, coming so quickly on the heels of the Bloody

Martov (Zederbaum), leader of the Menshevik faction.

Sunday incident, caught the party leadership by surprise. Lenin was in Geneva and he did not return to Petersberg until October—shortly before the Petersburg Soviet was organized. Martov the Menshevik leader, returned at the same time. Rosa Luxemberg arrived in December, by which time the insurrection had ended. Axelrod got only as far as Finland, and Plekhanov never returned at all. The 1905 revolution was principally led by second-string leaders, virtually all of whom were identified with the Mensheviks.

Trotzky alone of the top leadership had sensed the significance of "Bloody Sunday," and at the first word of revolution he and a Jewish compatriot, Parvus, had struck out for Petersberg.

Using the pseudonym Yanovsky, he very quickly became a leading member of the Soviet, and by the end of October was generally recognized as the most influential member of the Executive Committee. In addition, he edited (with Parvus) the Menshevik organ, Nachato. Later, under the pseudonym, "Peter Petrovich" he edited the "Russkyaya Gazeta." On Dec. 9, as we have previously related, he was elected president of the Petersberg Soviet, and following his arrest Parvus assumed leadership of the revolt.

Although Lenin had been in St. Petersburg throughout the life of the Petersberg Soviet, neither he nor any member of his faction played a prominent part in its activities. When the 300 members of the Soviet were finally arrested, not a single prominent Bolshevik was among them. The revolution of 1905 was strictly a Menshevik affair.

The London Congress

In 1907 (May 13 - June 1) a fifth Congress of the **Russian Social Democratic Labor Party** was held, this time in London. This was by all accounts the most impressive one of all, and it was the last one held before the 1917 revolution. Represented at the Congress were:

The Bolsheviks, led by Lenin—91 delegates.

The Mensheviks, led by Martov and Dan—89 delegates.

The Polish Social Democrats, led by Rosa Luxemberg—44 delegates.

The Jewish Bund, led by Rafael Abramovitch and M. I. Lieber—55 delegates.

The Lettish Social Democrats, led by "Comrade Herman" (Danishevsky).

Altogether there were 312 delegates to the Congress, of whom 116 were, or had been, workers. Dominating the Congress were the great names of the party: there were the founders of the movement, Plekhanov, Axelrod, Deutch, and Zasulich—who after 1907 played roles of diminishing importance in party affairs—and their disciples, Lenin, Martov, Dan (Gurvich), and Trotzky. There were Abramovich and Lieber (Goldman) of the Bund, and Rosa Luxemberg, the latter one day being destined to lead a revolution of her own in Germany. Present also were Zinoviev, Kamenev, and Stalin, none of whom were important in 1907, but who are listed here because one day they would be the three most powerful men in Russia. Significantly all of those named were Jewish, excepting Lenin, Plekhanov, and Stalin.

Perhaps one of the most important matters taken up by the **London Congress** was the bitterly controversial question of "expropriations." It should be explained that Lenin's Bolshevik faction had to an increasing degree resorted to outlawry to replenish its finances. Robbery. kidnapping, and theft became regular party activities. And on one occasion a loyal Bolshevik married a rich widow to secure funds for the party treasury. These activities were referred to in party circles as "expropriations." The most famous expropriation was the Tiflis bank robbery, engineered by young Josef Stalin shortly after the London Congress.

The Mensheviks bitterly criticized these tactics, while Lenin stoutly defended them as a necessary means of raising capital. The "expropriation" question broke out again and again as a point of contention between the two factions. Actually a great deal of Lenin's strength came from this source. With money thus raised he was able to pay the traveling expenses of delegates to these various congresses, and this gave him a voting power which was probably out of

In communist Russia the penalty for revolutionary activity is always death. Under the more tolerant rule of the Tsars the penalty was exile in Siberia. Stalin was exiled no less than 5 times. The photo above shows him with a friend (Suren Spandaryan) during exile in Monastryrskoye, Turukhansk, Siberia.

proportion to his following. Lenin's opposition on the expropriation question came not only from Martov's Menshevik faction, but also from the Jewish Bund and Rosa Luxemberg's Polish Social Democrats. The Jewish Bund and Rosa Luxemberg's faction usually sided with the Mensheviks in these intra-party squabbles. and it was not until 1917, when they were actually incorporated into the Bolshevik faction, that Lenin was able to actually control the entire party.

The Tiflis bank robbery has now become a part of the legend which surrounds Stalin, and it is perhaps worth while to give it some attention. Although the robbery was engineered by Stalin, then a minor party worker, the actual hold-up was carried out by an Armenian by the name of Petroyan, who is known in Russian history as "Kamo." Kamo's method was crude but effective: he tossed a dynamite bomb at a bank stage which was transporting 250,000 rubles in currency. In the resulting explosion some 30 people were killed and Kamo escaped with the loot, which consisted mainly of 500 ruble notes.

The Bolsheviks encountered considerable difficulty in converting these 500 ruble notes into usable form. It was decided that agents in various countries would simultaneously cash as many as possible in a single day. The operation was not a complete success. The Jewess, Olga Ravich, who was one day to marry Zinoviev was apprehended by police authorities, as was one Meyer Wallach, whose real name was Finklestein, and who is better known as Maxim Litinov. Litinov later became Commissar of Foreign Affairs (1930-39).

Litinov

The Year 1908

In the autumn of 1908 the Bolsheviks began publishing the **Proletariie**, with Lenin, Dubrovinsky, Zinoviev, and Kamenev (the latter two Jewish) as editors. In the same year the Menshevik organ, "**Golos Sotsial-Demokrata**" began publication, edited by Plekhanov, Axelrod, Martov, Dan, and Martynov (Pikel), all of whom were Jewish with the exception of Plekhanov. In Oct. of 1908 the **Vienna Pravda** was launched, with Trotzky as editor.

The Troika

In 1909 the Lenin-Zinoviev-Kamenev "**troika**" was formed. It was to endure until Lenin's death in 1924. Zinoviev and Kamenev were Lenin's inseparable companions. Later, when the Bolsheviks were in power, Trotzky would become co-equal with Lenin, and even something of a competitor, but Kamenev and Zinoviev were never Lenin's equals nor his competitors— they were his right and left hand. They would argue with him, and fight with him, and oppose him in party councils, but the "troika" was broken only when Lenin died.

January Plenum

In January of 1910 the 19 top leaders of the Party met in what historians refer to as the "**January Plenum of the Central Committee**." Its purpose was, as always, to promote party unity. One outcome was that Lenin was compelled to burn the remainder of the 500 ruble notes from the Tiflis expropriation, which he had been unable to cash anyway.

Zinoviev

Another outcome of the January Plenum was the recognition of the newspaper, **Sotsial Demokrata**, as the general party newspaper. Its editors were the Bolsheviks, Lenin and Zinoviev, and the Mensheviks, Martov and Dan. Trotzky's semi-independent "Vienna Pravda" was declared to be an official party organ, and Kamenev was appointed to help edit it. Who could have foretold in the year 1910 that within seven short years this Yiddish crew would be the lords and masters of all Russia?

The 1917 Revolution

The 1917 revolution, like that of 1905. caught the top leaders of the party unprepared. Lenin and Martov were in Switzerland, and Trotzky was eking out an existence in New York's East Side.

Shortly after the March revolution the German government did a peculiar thing. It arranged to ship Lenin, Martov, Radek, and 32 members of the party across Germany to Russia. The German strategy seemed to be based on the assumption—which later proved correct—that the communists would work to sabotage the Russian war effort, now being prosecuted by the Provisional Government. Perhaps the Lenin group had some such agreement with the Germans, no one knows. But one thing is certain: 48 hours after the Bolsheviks came to power, Trotzky began negotiations for an armistice. But that story comes later.

Kamenev

The Germans gave Lenin and party a sealed railway car.

Radek

On April 3rd, just 23 days after the provisional government had been formed, Lenin and his party arrived in Petersberg. Within 7 months he and his faction would be the supreme dictators of all Russia.

PETERSBERG SOVIET
It Controlled the Mob

We have already given a description of the March Revolution

which overthrew the Tsar, and we have told of the establishment of the two governing bodies which came into existence on March 12th, namely the Provisional Government and the Petersberg Soviet.

The Petersberg Soviet, formed on March 12th, was dominated by the Mensheviks under the leadership of the Jews, Lieber, Dan, and Martov. Later (in October) the Bolsheviks gained control when Trotzky became president, and they immediately precipitated the October Revolution.

The Petersberg Soviet, although it controlled the mob, was reluctant to assume the responsibility of governing—at least in the beginning. The Soviet was originally organized by second-string leaders who were quite capable of stirring up trouble, but who had little capacity for leading a revolutionary government. Furthermore, it was not clear in the early days of the revolution as to what the final outcome would be. Petersberg was, after all, only one city in the empire, and the attitude of the country as a whole, and of the soldiers at the front, was unknown. For this reason the Soviet preferred that the Provisional Government—which had some semblance of legitimacy—should temporarily rule.

The Provisional Government

The Provisional Government was not a revolutionary body. Of

its 12 members, only one, Kerensky, was a "Socialist." The others were typical upper-middle class members of the Duma, with possibly mild leanings to the left. Head of the Provisional Government was Prince Lvov, whose reputation as a liberal may have qualified him for that position more than some of the others. This 12 man government had sprung into being simply because no other semblance of a government existed in Petersberg on March 12th—it did not in any way

These twelve members of the Duma organized a Provisional Government under Prince Lvov. Later, in July, Kerensky took over.

Karl Radek, one of the "ready, self-confident men" who returned from exile to agitate for the Bolsheviks.

participate in the revolution. In the months following the overthrow of the Tsar, however, its power grew considerably, so that by July when an abortive Bolshevik uprising occurred, the Provisional Government was able to quell the affair and arrest or force into hiding the Bolshevik leaders.

The Provisional Government undertook to continue the war against Germany. The great mass of people were, of course, patriotic Russians, and Germany was looked on as a dangerous threat to Russian sovereignty. The Provisional Government, during its entire tenure, was primarily occupied with the prosecution of the war.

The Provisional Government took two steps, however, which were to profoundly affect the revolution. The first, and most fateful, was the decision to permit the return of all exiled political prisoners from Siberia and abroad. By doing so it sealed the fate of Russia. Here is the way one American writer, Edward Alworth Ross, has described it:

"**One of the first acts of the Provisional government, however, is to bring back to Russia the political victims of the autocracy. From Siberia about eighty thousand are brought out. From Switzerland, France, Scandinavia, the United States, even from Argentina and other remote countries, come perhaps ten thousand who** have been refugees from the tsar's vengeance. In all ninety thousand at least, virtually all of them of socialist sympathies, stream into European Russia in late April, May, June, and July. Honored by a grateful people for their voluntary sacrifices and sufferings they quickly rise to a commanding influence in the local soviets and carry them irresistibly toward the political left."[18]

These ninety thousand exiles constituted the heart of the approaching Bolshevik revolution. They were almost to the last man professional revolutionaries, and with few exceptions they were Jewish. Stalin, Sverdlov, and Zinoviev were among the exiles who returned from Siberia. Lenin, Martov, Radek, and Kamenev—as we have seen—returned from Switzerland. Trotzky returned, with hundreds of his Yiddish brethren, from New York's East Side. These were the inheritors of the revolution. Until their return the revolution had been without leadership—largely it had been conducted by second string leaders who happened to be on the spot. Now the elite were returning. Let us take another quotation from the starry-eyed Edward Alworth Ross, whose prose is almost as poor as his judgment: "**The bewildered leaderless Russian masses are thrilled and captivated by these ready, self-confident men who tell them just what they must do in order to garner for themselves the fruits of the revolution. This is why refugees, obscure to us although not to Russians, who in exile had been obliged to work in our steel mills and tailor shops for a living, former residents of New York's "Eastside," who lived precariously from some Russian newspapers we Americans never heard of, will rise to be the heads of soviets and, later, cabinet ministers of a government ruling a tenth of the human race. In all modern history there is no romance like it.**"[19]

Soon these hordes of returning Jews would exercise the power of life and death over 150 million Christian Russians. Soon every factory, every government bureau every school district, and every army unit would function under the gimlet eye of a Jewish Commissar. Soon the blood of human beings

---
18 Russian Bolshevik Revolution, page 58, by Edward Alsworth Ross, Century Company. New York. 1921
19 Russian Bolshevik Revolution (ibid p. 45), page 67

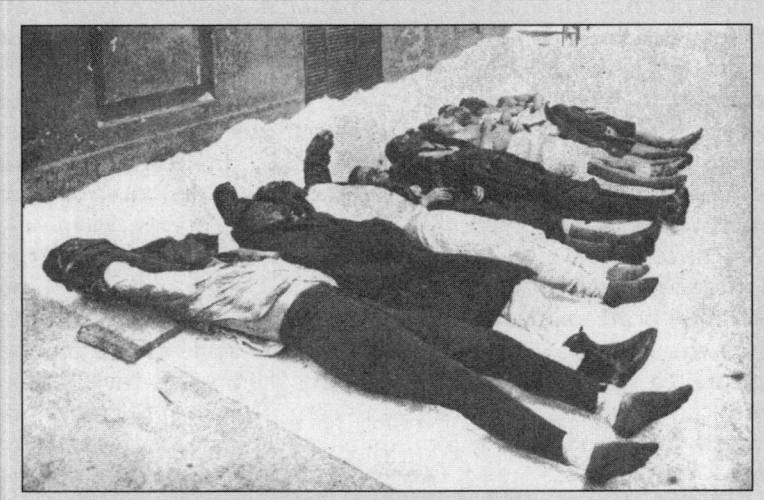

When the Bolsheviks came to power, they systematically undertook to destroy every vestige of opposition by exterminating the upper classes of Russian society. The fury of the Red Terror can be explained only as a manifestation of Jewish hatred against Christian civilization.

would be oozing from under the doors of communist execution chambers as tens of thousands of Christian men and women were butchered like cattle in a slaughterhouse. Soon five million landowners would be deliberately starved to death as part of a premeditated plan. Soon a move would be under way to exterminate the gentile leader class of the entire nation by murdering every Christian factory owner, and lawyer, and government leader, and army officer, and every other person who had been, or might be, a potential leader. Soon the standing population of the slave labor camps would exceed 15 million. Soon every church and cathedral would be gutted and every priest and preacher would become a criminal in his own community. Soon Russia would have a zombie-proletariat docile, willing to work, easily controlled, incapable of revolt... Such was the "romance" of the Bolshevik revolution.

When the Bolsheviks came to power, they systematically undertook to destroy every vestige of opposition by exterminating the upper classes of Russian society. The fury of the Red Terror can be explained only as a manifestation of Jewish hatred against Christian civilization.

Wherever communists have come to power, their first act has been to execute or imprison the nation's leader class. Their second act is to install Jews in every position of power and authority. In Russia literally millions of gentiles were butchered by Jew executioners.

Constituent Assembly Elections

A second important act of the Provisional Government was to create the machinery for the election of a **Constituent Assembly**. It was provided that delegates from all of Russia should be chosen in free elections, and these were to meet in a Constituent Assembly for the purpose of writing a constitution for Russia. It was to be, as one writer puts it:[20] **"a body encompassing the purposes of both the Continental Congress and the Constitutional Convention of the American Revolution."**

When the Constituent Assembly did meet, in January of 1918, the Bolsheviks had already been in power a month. **"It met at the Tauride Palace in Petrograd and lasted less than 13 hours; from four in the afternoon of Jan. 18, to 40 minutes past four of Jan. 19, when it was dispersed by Bolshevik troops, chiefly soldiers of Lettish regiments."** One of the factors which precipitated the October Revolution was the forthcoming elections for the Constituent Assembly.

[20] Stalin: An Appraisal of the Man and His Influence, by Lev Trotsky (translated by Charles Malamuth), Harper Bros., New York & London, 1941

All-Russian Congress of Soviets

One other event occurred which was to affect the outcome of the revolution. This was the convening of the **First All-Russian Congress of Soviets** in Petersberg on June 3rd, 1917. It should be explained that the word "soviet" means "council," or "committee." Following the March Revolution, literally hundreds of local revolutionary Soviets were organized all over Russia by the various Marxists parties. It was decided that a congress of these soviets should meet for the purpose of unifying the forces of the revolution.

This first Congress of Soviets was dominated by the Mensheviks and Essars. (**Essars = Social Revolutionary Party**). The Bolsheviks had fewer than 40 delegates out of several hundred attending.

Before disbanding, the Congress of Soviets set October 20th (later changed to Nov. 7th) as the date for the convening of the next Congress. This date is extremely important because it marks the date of the Bolshevik Revolution. When the Second Congress of Soviets did convene, on the evening of November 7th, the Bolsheviks had already gained control of the Petersberg Soviet and had overthrown the Provisional Government a few hours earlier. The Bolsheviks were thus able to present the **Second All-Russian Congress of Soviets** with a "fait accompli." This Second Congress of Soviets became the official government of Communist Russia on that same evening of November 7th, 1917.

Lenin Returns

But now we must turn our attention back to Lenin and his party at the time of their arrival from abroad. When Lenin arrived in Petersberg in April of 1917, he found the Petersberg Soviet dominated by the Mensheviks, with the Essars (Social Revolutionaries) second in membership, and the Bolsheviks in the minority. President of the Soviet was the Menshevik, Tcheidze, a "defensist" who strongly supported the war effort. Of the two vice-presidents, one was Skobelev, also a Menshevik, and the other was Kerensky, the only member of the 12 man Provisional Government who also belonged to the Soviet.

Although the Mensheviks controlled the Petersberg Soviet,

Immediately upon their arrival in Petersberg, the Bolsheviks, headed by Lenin (shown above addressing factory workers) began agitating against the Provisional Government. The Bolshevik slogan was "All Power to the Soviets." Eventually the Bolsheviks were able to win over the more radical elements of Petersberg's unstable industrial populations.

they were badly divided among themselves. The main body of the Menshevik faction—the defensists—was headed by Theodore Dan (Gurvich) and M. I. Lieber (formerly of the Jewish Bund). The other group of Mensheviks,—the internationalists—was headed by Martov.

Lenin bitterly criticized this state of affairs. He regarded the provisional government as an instrument of the "bourgeois" and he immediately and violently advocated its overthrow. Throughout April, May, and June the Bolsheviks preached the destruction of the Provisional Government, and among the factory workers and the military garrisons around Petersberg this propaganda began to take effect. Under the slogan **"all power to the Soviets,"** the Bol-

M. I. Lieber

Theodore Dan

The Petersburg Soviet was dominated by the Mensheviks until shortly before the Bolshevik revolt. The Mensheviks were divided among themselves, however, with Theodore Dan (above) and M.I. Lieber (preceding page), heading the "defensists," and Martov heading the "internationalists." All three were Jewish.

Because the Menshevik leadership was completely Jewish, while a number of gentiles were prominent among the Bolsheviks. Some Jewish propagandists have tried to portray the Bolshevik-Menshevik intra-party battle as a defeat for Jewish interests. Actually, it was more of a family fight between Jews. The Bolsheviks and Mensheviks, it should be remembered, were majority and minority factions of the same party. And both factions were completely Jewish controlled.

The caricatures of Lieber and Dan are taken from an official communist history book.

sheviks had succeeded by July in recruiting to their banners large numbers of the city's more radical elements.

The returning influx of exiles also enhanced the position of the Bolsheviks. These exiles were not all originally Bolsheviks, but they were almost without exception extremists, and they had waited a long time for revolution to come: they were hungry for power. And they were inclined to favor the Bolsheviks because they were the most radical advocates of direct action. Trotzky, who had in 1905 began a Menshevik, and who had later been a "neutral," immediately joined the Bolsheviks on his return from New York. So it was with many others.

On July 17th this anti-government agitation resulted in an unscheduled uprising by thousands of the city's inflamed worker-soldier population. In modern Russian history these are known as the "July Days." Kerensky, who by now had become the dominant figure in the Provisional Government dealt with the insurrection with considerable firmness. The mob was fired on, and in the course of the next three days several hundred people were killed.

As a result of the **"July Days"** uprising, the top Bolshevik leadership was either arrested or forced to flee. Lenin and Zinoviev temporarily hid out in Sestroretsk, outside of Petersberg. Trotzky, Kamenev, and Lunacharsky (soon to

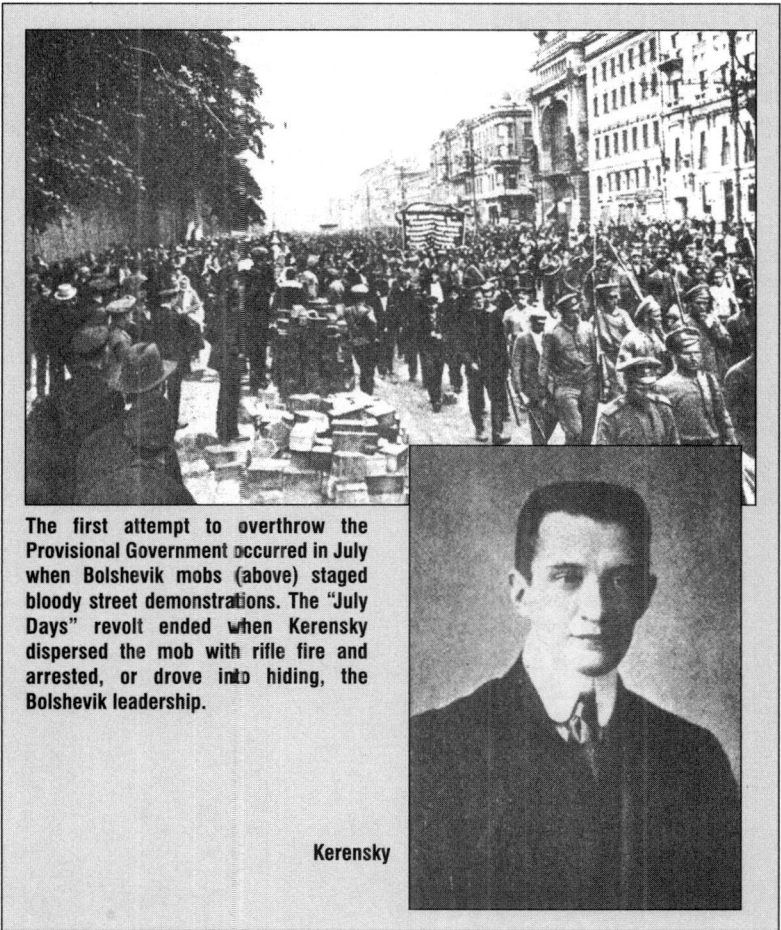

The first attempt to overthrow the Provisional Government occurred in July when Bolshevik mobs (above) staged bloody street demonstrations. The "July Days" revolt ended when Kerensky dispersed the mob with rifle fire and arrested, or drove into hiding, the Bolshevik leadership.

Kerensky

become prominent) were arrested. Stalin, at that time an editor of Pravda, was not molested.

One result of the "July Days" was the collapse of the Provisional Government under the premiership of Prince Lvov. On July 20th, Kerensky (Adler) the Jewish Napoleon, became Prime Minister of a 'salvation of the revolution' government. Kerensky was quite an orator, and he applied himself to the task of whipping up enthusiasm for an offensive against the Germans. Although he met with moderate success at first, the offensive failed and Kerensky's influence declined steadily in the next three months.

Sixth Party Congress

In August (8-16) the Russian Social-Democratic Labor Party held its Sixth Congress. This was the first one held since the **London Congress of 1907**, and it was the last one held before the Bolshevik Revolution, now only two months away. This Sixth Congress was completely a Bolshevik affair. The other factions merged with the Bolsheviks and ceased to exist; from this time on the Russian Social Democratic Labor Party WAS the Bolshevik Party. (Within a year the party

Petersberg mob scene during the "July Days."

officially changed its name to the Communist Party).

The most important act of the Sixth Congress was to elect the **"October Central Committee,"** consisting of 26 members. This Central Committee was to rule the Bolshevik Party through the critical days of the October Revolution. Who were the principal members of the "October Central Committee"? Let us take the words of Lev Trotzky as they appear in his book, Stalin:[21] "In view of the Party's semi-legality the names of persons elected by secret ballot were not announced at the Congress, with the exception of the four who had received the largest number of votes. Lenin—133 out of a possible 134, Zinoviev—132, Kamenev—131, Trotzky—131."[22] These four two months before the October Revolution, were the top leaders of the Bolshevik Party. All were Jews and Lenin was married to a Jewess.

Trotzky's writings are extremely enlightening from a historical viewpoint. He hated Stalin and he wrote his book, Stalin, to prove that Stalin was a Johnny-come-lately, an upstart, and an usurper. He brings forth masses of evidence to show how unimportant Stalin was in Party councils during and immediately after the October Revolution. In doing so, Trotzky again and again emphasizes who the really important leaders were. Let us take another typical comment from his book on Stalin as he describes the meetings of the October Central Committee shortly before the Bolshevik Revolution:

"The 422 pages of the fourth volume, dealing with August and September, record all the happenings, occurrences, brawls, resolutions, speeches, articles in any way deserving of notice. Sverdlov, then practically unknown, was mentioned three times in that volume; Kamenev, 46 times; I, who spent August and the beginning of September in prison, 31 times; Lenin, who was in the underground, 16 times; Zinoviev, who shared Lenin's fate, 6 times. Stalin was not mentioned even once. Stalin's name is not even in the index of approximately 500 proper names."

Thus, Trotzky again cites evidence to prove that Stalin was not an important figure in the Bolshevik Party in 1917. But in doing so he names the real leaders, who as before are the Jews, Kamenev, Zinoviev, Trotzky, and the up and coming

---
21 Stalin (ibid) pages 220-221
22 Stalin (ibid) pages 222-223

The above cut is taken from Trotzky's book, "Stalin." It is a reproduction of a postcard widely circulated in Russia following the Bolshevik Revolution. It is entitled "Leaders of the Proletarian Revolution." Trotzky uses this as evidence to prove that Stalin, whom he despised, was not an important figure in the October Revolution—which it does nicely. But it also reveals the Jewishness of these original leaders of the Communist Party: All six of the above are Jews. Shown above are (1) Lenin, (2) Trotzky, (3) Zinoviev, (4) Lunacharsky, (5) Kamenev, (6) Sverdlov. These were the leaders of the Communist Revolution of 1917.

Sverdlov. Lenin is the only gentile.

Because the top party leaders were either in prison or in hiding as a result of the abortive July Days uprising, the Sixth Party Congress was organized by the lesser lights of the party, of whom Sverdlov was the most active. Lev Trotzky, ever anxious to discredit Stalin, gives us this description:[23] **"The praesidium consisted of Sverdlov, Olminsky, Lomov, Yurenev, and Stalin. Even here, with the most prominent figures of Bolshevism absent, Stalin's name is listed in last place. The Congress resolved to send greetings to 'Lenin, Trotzky, Zinoviev, Lunacharsky, Kamenev, Kollontai, and all the others arrested and persecuted comrades.' These were elected to the honorary praesidium."**

Here again, in the words of Trotzky, we have named the "most prominent figures of Bolshevism:" Lenin, Trotzky, Zinoviev, Kamenev, Kollontai and Lunacharsky. And we know these were the most important leaders because they were the ones Kerensky had arrested or driven underground following the July Days revolt. Of these, only Lunacharsky was gentile; the others were Jewish. These facts show why the Jewishness of communism is so immediately and indisputably apparent to anyone who has the slightest knowledge of Bolshevik history.

* TROTZKY TO POWER *

On August 17th Kamenev was released from prison, and exactly a month later Trotzky was also freed by the Kerensky regime. On Sept. 24th Trotzky was elected president of the Petersberg Soviet, displacing Cheidze, the Menshevik. From this moment on the Bolsheviks were in control of the Petersberg Soviet. On October 29th the Petersberg Soviet voted to transfer all military power to a **"Military Revolutionary Committee,"** headed by Trotzky. Revolution was now only days away.

Military Revolutionary Committee

The Military Revolutionary Committee, under the chairmanship of Trotzky, was organized for the express purpose of preparing

---
23 Stalin (ibid) page 217.

Headquarters of the Military Revolutionary Committee during the October Revolution was Smolny Institute. From here Trotzky commanded the forces which overthrew the Kerensky regime.

The fate of Kerensky's regime was sealed when the Bolsheviks stormed the Winter Palace, last redoubt of the Provisional Government. Kerensky managed to escape, later fled to Paris.

the revolution. Time was running out and it was a matter of striking soon or not at all. The Constituent Assembly elections were only a few weeks off, and when it convened, Russia was to have a new government. There was another reason for striking soon. The Second All-Russian Congress of Soviets was to meet on Nov. 7th. The Bolsheviks feared—and with reason—that the Kerensky government would arrest or disband the entire congress and thereby doom the revolt. For these reasons it was felt essential to overthrow the Provisional Government by or before the Second All-Russian Congress of Soviets convened on Nov. 7th.

On November 4th the Military Revolutionary Committee arranged huge mass meetings in preparation for the forthcoming revolt. On the following day the garrison of the Peter and Paul Fortress declared itself in alliance with the Bolsheviks. On the 6th Kerensky made one last attempt to forestall revolution by ordering the arrest of the Military Revolution Committee, banning all Bolshevik publications, and ordering fresh troops to replace the Petersberg garrison. These measures were never carried out.

Revolution

On the evening of November 6th Lenin came out of hiding and joined the Military Revolutionary Committee at Smolny Institute which served as revolutionary headquarters. At two A.M. the following morning the revolution began.

By noon the city was largely in Bolshevik hands. At three P.M. Lenin delivered a fiery speech to the Petersberg Soviet—his first since July. At nine P.M. Bolshevik troops began their two day siege of the Winter Palace, last stronghold of the Provisional Government.

At eleven P. M. the Second All-Russian Congress of Soviets convened with the Bolsheviks in a clear majority. The Congress was now the official government of Russia. The Jew Kamenev, was elected its first President. Lenin became Premier. Trotzky was made Commissar of Foreign Affairs. Before dawn it had elected a Central Executive Committee under the chairmanship of Kamenev, who thus had the distinction of being the first President of the "Soviet Republic."

Within a few days (Nov. 21) the Jew, Sverdlov, succeeded

Kamenev, and thus became the second Jewish president of the "Soviet Republic." A relatively minor figure in Bolshevik circles six months before the revolution, he very quickly became one of the five top men in the party.

Before his early death two years later he had become the party's chief trouble-shooter and had assumed absolute control over Russia's economic life.

Yakov Sverdlov

CONSTITUENT ASSEMBLY

On November 25th, 8 days after the Bolshevik coup, free elections were held throughout Russia under machinery set up by the Provisional Government. The Bolsheviks, not yet completely organized, made no attempt to interfere with the elections, but when it became clear that the Bolsheviks would command only a minority in the Constituent Assembly, they immediately laid plans to undermine its authority.

The Provisional Government had specified that the convocation of the Assembly should be in the hands of a special commission. The Bolsheviks arrested this commission, and substituted for it a "Commissary for the Constituent Assembly," headed by the Jew, Uritzky.

Uritzky

By this tactic the Bolsheviks were able to exert their authority over the Assembly. When the Assembly did finally convene, the Jew, Sverdlov, although not a delegate, took charge of the proceedings, and actually called the meeting to order. Ten hours later the Assembly was thrown into confusion when the Bolsheviks walked out. Shortly thereafter Bolshevik troops brutally brought the Constituent Assembly to an end by ejecting the delegates and locking the

BEHIND COMMUNISM 〇 73

doors to the building.

This was the end of the Constituent Assembly. After having convened for only 13 hours, it disbanded, never to meet again. So ended Russia's hope for a constitution and a representative government.

In March, 1918, the Soviet Government moved its capital from Petersberg to Moscow. In the same month the **Russian Social-Democratic Labor Party officially styled itself the Communist Party...**

War Commissar

Meanwhile the enemies of the new regime were gathering strength. Before the year was over the Soviet Government was under attack on six war fronts. Some of these anti-communist armies were organized by pro-Tsarist sympathizers; others were organized and financed by foreign governments. These "White Russian" forces constituted a dangerous threat to the new regime, and in March Trotzky relinquished his post as Commissar of Foreign Affairs to become Commissar of War, a position which gave him authority over the Soviet Government's entire military resources. It was he who

Lev Trotzky (above center) is shown at the height of his power as Commissar of War. It was Trotzky who organized the Red Army and led it to victory over the White Russian Armies.

organized and led the Red Army to victory Not until 1921 were the last of the anti-communist forces destroyed.

Murder of the Royal Family

Shortly after the March Revolution of 1917 the Tsar had applied for permission for himself and his family to leave the country. Nicholas II was closely related to the royal families of England and Denmark, and he felt exile there was preferable to remaining a prisoner in his own land. The Provisional Government had been inclined to grant his request, but the Petersberg Soviet had blocked the move and the royal family had been transferred to Ekaterinburg, in south Russia. There, in 1918, they were housed in the home

The above is a reproduction of a banner displayed by the Bolsheviks on the first anniversary of the Communist Revolution. After having butchered the royal family and a substantial part of the nation's ruling class, the Bolsheviks set out to "educate" the Russian people to the joys of proletarian life. So successful has this program of "education" been, that the enslaved Russian people actually believe they are privileged to live under Jew-Communism. The above poster, incidentally, again reveals the Jewishness of the Communist leadership: of the twelve shown, six are Jews and one (Lenin) is married to a Jewess. To the right of Lenin: Pokrovsky, Kamenev*, Sverdlov*, Lunacharsky, Kollontai, Krylenko, Zinoviev*, Bukharin, Trotzky*, Rykov, Radek*.
*NOTE: On a previous page Mme. Kollontai is inadvertently identified as Jewish. Her nationality is unverified.

of a local merchant named Ipatiev. On July 17th anti-Bolshevik troops advanced on Ekaterinburg and the local commissar, a Jew by the name of Yorovsky, ordered the family—and their household servants—executed. Yorovsky personally dispatched Nicholas with a pistol shot in the head. The rest of the family was executed by a firing squad. Their bodies were then soaked in oil and burned...

Should the reader be moved to look up the position of Ekaterinburg on a modern day map of Soviet Russia, he will find no trace of it. The former city and province of Ekaterinburg has been renamed "Sverdlovsk," in honor of the Jew, Yakov Sverdlov, president of the "Soviet Republic" at the time of the execution...

THE RED TERROR

On August 30, 1918, the Jew, Uritzky—then head of the "Cheka"—was assassinated and Lenin was wounded. The assassins were both Jewish, and both members of the Jewish-led Social Revolutionary Party. The Bolsheviks used this as an excuse for instituting the Red Terror, which began the following day, and which in a sense has continued to the present.

Space simply does not permit us to give an adequate description of what followed. The entire membership of the Communist Party, which in 1918 numbered perhaps no more than 100,000, was turned into an instrument of murder. Its aims were two-fold; to inspire dread and horror among the Russian masses, and to exterminate the middle and upper classes i.e., the "bourgeois."

Men and women were executed or imprisoned not because of any offense, but simply because they belonged to the "enemy class." And this definition eventually included every merchant, professional person and landowner. Not only were these "class enemies" exterminated, but members of their families fell victim as well. The Bolsheviks cleverly adopted the practice of making hostages of the families of those who resisted the new order. David Shub in his slavishly pro-Marxist book, "Lenin," gives the following description of the Red Terror in Petersberg:[24] **"Little time was wasted**

---
[24] Lenin, (abridgement by Donald P. Geddes), page 156, by David Shub, New American Library, 1950 (Mentor Books).

sifting evidence and classifying people rounded up in these night raids. Woe to him who did not disarm all suspicion at once. The prisoners were generally hustled to the old police station not far from the Winter Palace. Here, with or without perfunctory interrogation, they were stood up against the courtyard wall and shot. The staccato sounds of death were muffled by the roar of truck motors kept going for the purpose." This was the Red Terror in action.

The tragedy of all this cannot be measured by numbers alone; these people were the best that Russia had. They were the leader class. They were the priests, and lawyers, and merchants, and army officers, and university professors. They were the cream of Russian civilization.

The total effect was much the same as it would be in any country. With its small middle and upper class exterminated, Russia's peasant and worker population accepted Jewish Bolshevism without protest. The Russian masses, deprived of its spokesmen and leaders was simply incapable of counter-revolution. That was what the Red Terror set out to accomplish...

The Third International

A basic tenet of Marxist ideology was, and is, the promotion of world revolution. The Bolshevik leadership undertook in 1919 to further this aim by establishing the Third International, which convened in March of 1919. Its presiding officer was Lenin, and its first president was the Jew, Zinoviev, who remained its head until 1926.

The prime objective of the Third International was to establish communist parties in the various countries of the world, and to lend them aid and assistance in overthrowing their respective governments. Prospects of success were bright in the spring of 1919...

Rosa Luxemberg's Revolution

The first country to experience a communist revolution outside of Russia was Germany. The German government, which had abetted the Bolshevik coup in 1917 by facilitating Lenin's return to Russia via the sealed railway car, was in

1918 faced with a revolution of its own.

In many respects the German Revolution paralleled the one in Russia. As World War I reached the climatic year of 1918, and as German manpower losses mounted, the Jew-dominated German Social Democratic Party spread the seeds of defeatism among the German population much as the Bolsheviks had done in Russia. On November 3rd a mutiny broke out in the navy at Kiel, followed by rioting by the Social Democrats. On November 9th the Kaiser renounced his throne and the Social Democrats proclaimed a Socialist Republic. Two days later, on Nov. 11th, they agreed to an Armistice with the Allies.

There now occurred an event which was to embitter the German people against the Jews for all time, and which eventually resulted in the rise of Adolf Hitler. This was the demobilization of the German armies. It should be explained that Germany did not surrender by the terms of the November 11th Armistice; the agreement was that all German armies were to withdraw to the pre-war boundaries of Germany as a preliminary to a negotiated peace. But as the German armies retreated to German soil, the Revolutionary government, fearful lest the Revolution be upset, ordered them demobilized. On November 11th Germany still possessed the mightiest military machine on earth; thirty days later it had nothing. Instead of being able to negotiate peace on the terms of Wilson's Fourteen Points, a helpless and prostrate Germany got the Versailles Treaty....

Rosa Luxemburg

No sooner had the German armies been demobilized than the more extreme elements of the Social Democratic Party, led by Rosa Luxemberg, laid plans to seize control of the revolution as the Bolsheviks had done in Russia. Aided by funds provided by the Soviet ambassador Joffe, Rosa Luxemberg's "Spartacus Bund" in January of 1919 attempted to overthrow the revolutionary government. The revolt, following bloody street fighting, was quelled and its leaders, Rosa Luxemberg and Karl Liebknecht, were imprisoned and later executed by German army officers. Following the execution of Rosa Luxemberg, the Third International dispatched the Jew, Karl Radek, to lead the party. Later the Jewess, Ruth Fischer, assumed control of the German communist party, and remained at its head till 1924.

Bela Kun

Following World War I, Hungary also had a communist Revolution. in this case the instigator was the Jew, Bela Kun (Cohen), who imposed a communist regime on the country in the spring of 1919. Bela Kun had participated in the Bolshevik Revolution in Russia, and following the Armistice, he and a group of Jewish revolutionaries, using forged passports, moved into Hungary and established the communist newspaper, Voros Ursay (Red News). Well supplied with finances by the Soviet government, and aided by the pro-communist resident Jewish population, Kun quickly became the dictator of all Hungary.

Bela Kun proceeded to follow the pattern of the Bolshevik revolution. Says Encyclopedia Britannica:[25] **"Kun's programme was to 'arm at once, and forcibly transfer every industry and all landed property without conservation into the hands of the proletariat.' At first he collaborated with the Social Democrats but soon shouldered them aside, nationalized all banks, all concerns with over 200 employees, all landed property over 1000 ac., every**

Bela Kun

[25] Encyclopedia Britannica, page 517, vol. 13-1946

building other than workmen's dwellings. All jewelry, all private property above the minimum (e.g. two suits, 4 shirts, 2 pair of boots and 4 socks) was seized; servants abolished, bathrooms made public on Saturday nights; priests, with the insane, criminals and shopkeepers, employing paid assistants were declared incapable of the active or passive suffrage."

The result of this program was, as in Russia, economic and social chaos. The nationalization of every private bathroom in a country cannot be accomplished without profoundly affecting the social and moral tone of its society. Neither can the land, buildings, and industries of a nation be nationalized without creating havoc. As in Russia, such a program could only be enforced by resorting to the Red Terror. During Bela Kun's three month reign of terror, tens of thousands of people—priests, army officers, merchants, landowners, professional people—were butchered.

The communizing of the country's industrial and agricultural resources produced a famine in the cities, and this, combined with the peasantry's antipathy for the Jews, resulted in Kun's eventual overthrow. In an amazingly frank report, the New International Year Book of 1919 (Dodd, Mead, Co., page 587) has summarized the situation: **"One of the chief weaknesses in the new regime was antipathy to the Jews. In the country districts the feeling was widespread that the revolution had been a movement on the part of the Jews to seize the power for themselves, and the remark was frequently heard that if the Jews of Budapest died of starvation, so much the better for the rest of the country. The government of Bela Kun was composed almost exclusively of Jews who held also the administrative offices. The communist had united at first with the socialists who were not of the extremely radical party, but resembled somewhat the Labor parties or trade unionists groups in other countries. Bela Kun did not, however select his personnel from among them, but turned to the Jews and constituted virtually a Jewish bureaucracy."**

After three months of blood, murder, and pillage, Bela Kun Was deposed and interned in a lunatic asylum. Later he was released and returned to Russia, where he assumed control of the Red Terror organization the Cheka, in South Russia.

The Triumvirate

Lenin died of a brain hemorrhage in January of 1924. By this time the communists had become firmly entrenched. The civil wars were over and every vestige of organized resistance to Jewish-Bolshevism had been destroyed. On Lenin's death the party leadership fell to fighting among itself.

Lenin had, as early as May of 1922 suffered a paralytic stroke which affected his speech and motor reflexes. In December he suffered a second stroke, and his place was taken by a triumvirate composed of Zinoviev, Kamenev, and Joseph Stalin. Shortly afterwards Lenin suffered another stroke, and in 1924 he died.

Trotzky in Decline

In the early days of the new regime Trotzky had enjoyed near equality with Lenin in prestige and power. Outside of Russia, Lenin-Trotzky were regarded as a duality, and in current literature of that period their names were often hyphenated. The outside world had therefore fully expected Trotzky to assume Lenin's mantle as party leader. But after 1922 Trotzky's prestige in the Politburo had declined rapidly, as we shall see.

In the year the triumvirate began to function the Politburo was composed of Lenin, Zinoviev, Kamenev, Trotzky, Bukharin, Tomsky, and Stalin. The Lenin-Zinoviev-Kamenev "troika" had, of course, been dominant so long as Lenin was active, but now Zinoviev and Kamenev, as the surviving members of the "troika," regarded themselves as Lenin's rightful successors, and they looked on Trotzky as a competitor. Into this picture Stalin insinuated himself. He allied himself with Kamenev and Zinoviev, and the three were able to turn the Politburo against Trotsky. Stalin thus became the junior member of the triumvirate. Trotsky describes the situation this way:[26] **"Used as a counterweight against me, he was bolstered and encouraged by Zinoviev and Kamenev, and to a lesser extent by Rykov, Bukharin**

---
[26] Stalin (ibid page 48) page 337

and Tomsky. No one thought at the time that Stalin would some day loom away above their heads. In the first triumvirate Zinoviev treated Stalin in a circumspectly patronizing manner; Kamenev with a touch of irony."

Zinoviev was considered to be the senior triumvir, and he gave the opening address at the 12th Party Congress, a function heretofore reserved to Lenin. Zinoviev was not well received in this capacity, and before the Congress had adjourned, Stalin's control over the party machine gave him a dominant position in the triumvirate. This was the situation shortly after Lenin's death.

Stalin to Power

Stalin now moved to consolidate his position. In April of 1925 he engineered Trotzky's removal as War Commissar. In the same month he broke with Zinoviev and Kamenev and allied himself with politburo members Bukharin, Rykov, and Tomsky

Trotzky, Zinoviev, and Kamenev now united their forces in opposition to Stalin. But now it was too late. In February of 1926 Zinoviev was expelled from the Politburo then from the presidency of the Petersberg (Leningrad) Soviet, and finally as president of the Third International. Less than a month later (October 23) Trotzky and Kamenev were also expelled from the Politburo.

This marked the end of any effective resistance to Stalin. The next year Zinoviev, Kamenev, and Trotzky were removed from the party's Central Committee, and shortly afterwards all three were read out of the party. In 1929 Trotzky was exiled abroad. In June of 1930 Stalin became the supreme dictator of Russia.

It is frequently argued that Stalin's rise to power marked the end of the Jewish phase of communism. In support of this, it is pointed out that while such Jews as Trotzky, Zinoviev, Kamenev, Martynov, Zasulich, Deutsch, Parvus, Axelrod, Radek, Uritzky, Sverdlov, Dan, Lieber, Martov, and others were prominent in the early history of the revolution, these have almost without exception been executed or exiled. This on the surface is a convincing argument. But it completely overlooks the fact that Stalin has both a Jewish wife and a Jewish son-in-law. Both Stalin and his daughter, Svetlana, have married into the powerful Jewish Kaganovich family.

* STALIN'S PAST *

Some authors have suggested that Stalin is himself a Jew. Known facts do not bear this out. Stalin (born Joseph Vissarionovich Djugashvili) was born in the mountain village of Gori, situated in the province of Georgia, in 1879. His father, Vissarion Djugashvili, was a peasant from the neighboring town of Dido-Lilo—his mother was Ekaterina Geladze, whose forebears were serfs in the village of Gambareuli.

Not too much is known about Stalin's father. He was for a time a cobbler, and he seems to have worked as a day laborer

Young Stalin (inset) attended this elementary school in Gori. Although not as well educated as other red leaders such as Lenin and Trotzky, he was better schooled than most gentile Russians.

in a shoe factory in Adelkhanov. He is said to have been a heavy drinker.

Stalin's mother was a devoutly religious woman who took in washing to feed her family, and her life's ambition was to see her son become a priest. Young "Stalin" attended the elementary school in Gori—a four year course—and in 1894 he obtained a free scholarship to the Tiflis Theological

Seminary which provided free clothing, books, and food in addition to his tuition. Four years later he was expelled, after which he applied himself to revolutionary activity.

Stalin's first wife was Ekaterina Svanidze, who bore him one son (Yasha Jacob) Dugashvili. Jacob was a dullard who, even after his father became dictator, worked as an electrician and a railway mechanic.

Vasili Stalin

Stalin's second wife was Nadya Alliluyeva, who bore him a son, Vasili, and a daughter, Svetlana. Vasili is now a major-general in the Red Air Force.

Svetlana Stalin has been married twice. Nothing is known of her first husband—we do not even know when the marriage occurred. or where, or who the groom was. It is an official government secret.

A rare photo of Stalin's daughter, Svetlana, as a child. She is now married to the Jew, Mihail Kaganovich, son of politburo member, Lazar Kaganovich. Stalin's wife is Rosa Kaganovich.

Svetlana Stalin Marries Kaganovich

The fate, as well as the identity of Svetlana's first husband remains unknown. But of her second husband there is no doubt whatever: he is Mihail Kaganovich, son of Politburo minister Lazar Kaganovich and he is a Jew.

This leads one to speculate as to the true position of Lazar Kaganovich in Russia today. With a daughter married to Stalin, and a son married to Stalin's only daughter, he is to say the least, in a unique position. Just where Stalin's power leaves off and Kagan-ovich's begins is difficult to determine....

KAGANOVICH

One of the most frequent arguments used to disprove the Jewishness of Russia's present day leadership, strangely enough, revolves around Lazar Kaganovich. Propagandists are fond of

The excerpt is taken from Life magazine (July 14, 1941). It identifies Lazar Kaganovich as (1) "probably the ablest man on the politburo;" (2) Stalin's brother-in-law; (3) "the most eligible looking member of the politburo;" (4) a Jew. Facts like these are considered "anti-semitic," are seldom printed by the American press.

Svetlana Stalin's elaborate marriage to Mihail Kaganovich was reported by the Associated Press on July 15, 1951. Facts concerning the origins of Soviet rulers are not only censored in Russia, but in the U.S. as well. Any American publication revealing that Stalin has a Jewish wife and a Jewish son-in-law would be accused of "bigotry" and "hate mongering."

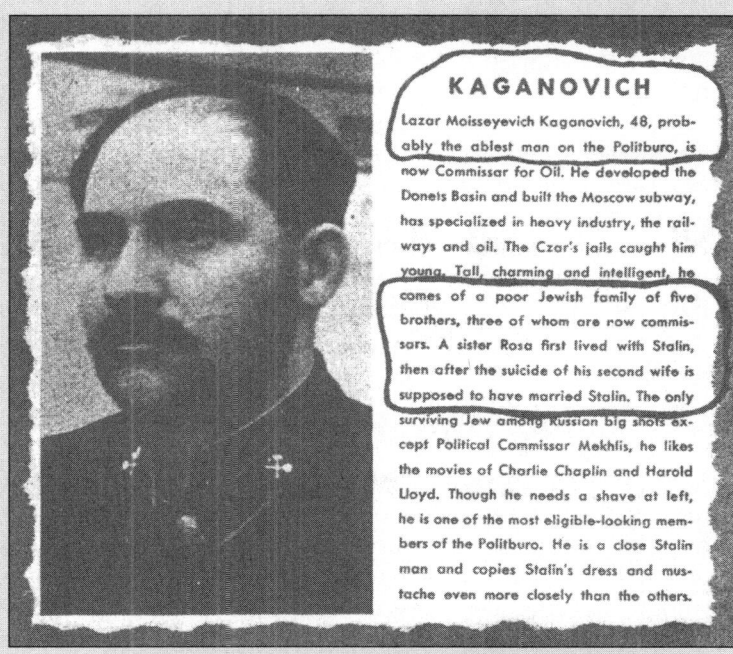

KAGANOVICH

Lazar Moisseyevich Kaganovich, 48, probably the ablest man on the Politburo, is now Commissar for Oil. He developed the Donets Basin and built the Moscow subway, has specialized in heavy industry, the railways and oil. The Czar's jails caught him young. Tall, charming and intelligent, he comes of a poor Jewish family of five brothers, three of whom are now commissars. A sister Rosa first lived with Stalin, then after the suicide of his second wife is supposed to have married Stalin. The only surviving Jew among Russian big shots except Political Commissar Mekhlis, he likes the movies of Charlie Chaplin and Harold Lloyd. Though he needs a shave at left, he is one of the most eligible-looking members of the Politburo. He is a close Stalin man and copies Stalin's dress and mustache even more closely than the others.

The above excerpt is taken from Life magazine, July 14, 1941.

Molotov's wife is the sister of the Jew, Sam Karp, owner of the Karp Export-Import Co., Bridgeport, Connecticut.

Svetlana Molotov, half-Jewish daughter of Russia's vice-premier, was betrothed to Vassili Stalin when this picture was taken in 1951.

pointing him out as "the only Jewish member of the Politburo," the suggestion being that since the Politburo contains only one Jew, it is plainly not Jewish controlled. But this argument will not stand the light of day it completely ignores the fact that both Premier Stalin and vice-premier Molotov have Jewish wives. And it conveniently overlooks the fact that the solitary Jew, Kaganovich, is doubly related to Stalin by marriage. Kaganovich is not just another member of the Politbureau he is Stalin's brother-in-law, and his chief advisor and trouble-shooter. The Stalin-Molotov-Kaganovich combination which rules Russia today is just as solidly Jewish as was the original Lenin-Zinoviev-Kamenev-Trotzky government.

IRON CURTAIN DICTATORS

In the communist satellite nations, as in Russia, the Jews occupy virtually every key position of power. Perhaps no better proof of this can be found than in John Gunther's book, "Behind the Iron Curtain."[27] Gunther, a Jew-Loving "liberal" of the most sickening type, reveals that Poland, Hungary, Roumania, and Czechoslovakia all have Jewish Dictators (see cut). Given here is a brief description of these "Iron Curtain Dictators."

> munists, and take part in their administrations.
> 10. Jews play a very prominent role in several governments. Here we tread delicate ground. The three "Muscovites" who run Hungary are Jews, the men who dominate Poland are Jews, the secretary general of the Communist party in Czechoslovakia is a Jew, Ana Pauker of Rumania is a Jewess. This brings up the grave point that Jews, as a race and a nation, may be unjustly assessed blame—by the ignorant—for the nature of these

The above excerpt is taken from page 40 of John Gunther's "Behind the Iron Curtain." Later in the book Gunther identifies "the three Muscovites who run Hungary," as the Jews, Rakosi, Vas, and Gero. He also identifies the Jew who runs Poland as Jacob Berman, and reveals that the Jewish general secretary of the party in Czechoslovakia is Rudolph Slansky. In spite of all this, Gunther vigorously denies Communism is Jewish.

---

27 Behind the Iron Curtain - page 40 by John Gunther, Harper & Brothers, New York.

HUNGARY: The three "moscovites" mentioned by Gunther (above), are the Jews, Matyas Rakosi (Rosencranz), Erno Gero (Singer), and Zoltan Vas. Hungary has enjoyed the unique privilege of undergoing two bloody communist dictatorships, both Jewish-led. The first was that of Bela Kun. When Kun's regime collapsed in 1919, hundreds of his Jewish compatriots fled with him to Russia, among whom were Matyas Rakosi and Erna Gera.

Matyas Rakosi

In 1945, when the communist took over the country, Matyas Rakosi was installed as the supreme dictator of Hungary, with Erno Gera and Zoltan Vas occupying positions number two and three.

Rakosi is an intimate of Stalin, knew Lenin personally, and was Commissar of Social Production under Bela Kun. He is a typical member of the Jewish bureaucracy which controls communism.

Although every foreign correspondent and every news service knows the identity of these "Iron Curtain" dictators, they are seldom in the press, and never are they identified as Jews. Any newspaperman daring to identify the communist leadership as Jewish would instantly be threatened with loss of advertising, and would be accused of "bigotry" and "anti-Semitism."

POLAND: Poland has shared the tragic fate of Hungary. "The men who dominate Poland" (See Gunther's cut, preceding page) are the Jews, Minc, Skryeszewski, Modzelewski, and Berman. The first three are of cabinet rank, while Jacob Berman's official position is that of Under-Secretary of State—a minor office. Yet it is this Jacob Berman who is the undisputed boss of Poland.

Berman, a product of the Warsaw ghetto, has lived in Russia, and was installed as dictator over Poland when the Russian armies took over the country. He prefers to work

Jacob Berman

behind the scenes as much as possible—a device frequently used to hide the Jewishness of communism. Poland's Jewish bureaucracy is perhaps the largest of my Iron Curtain country outside of Russia proper. Although Jews comprise less than 3% of the total population behind the Iron Curtain, they occupy virtually every position of authority. These facts should convince even the most doubtful that communism is Jewish—that behind international communism stands the international Jew. Jews and communists will never bother to deny this, but they will viciously attack those who expose the truth.

ROUMANIA: Anna Pauker, well known as the boss of Roumania, is so obviously Jewish, and so well recognized as such, that documentation is unnecessary.

Anna was born in Bucharest of orthodox Jewish parents. Her father (who was a Kosher butcher) and a brother now live in Israel. Anna earned a living for a time teaching Hebrew, and for a while she lived in the U.S. Her husband became identified as a "Trotskyite," and was executed in one of Stalin's purges. Today Anna Pauker is one of the most powerful figures in the communist world.

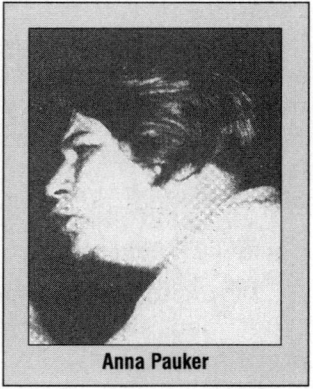
Anna Pauker

YUGOSLAVIA: The only non-Jewish dictator behind the Iron Curtain is Tito of Yugoslavia, which fact probably explains his revolt against the Kremlin. But Tito was tutored by the Jew, Mosa Pijade. Says John Gunther of Pijade: "He is Tito's mentor... Whatever ideological structure Tito may have, he got from this shrewd old man."[28]

---

28 Behind the Iron Curtain, by John Gunther, Harper Brothers, New York.

CZECHOSLOVAKIA: The secretary-general of the communist party in Czechoslovakia, whom John Gunther identifies as a Jew dictator, is Rudolph Slansky. Like the other satellite dictators, he was placed in command of things when the communists took over. Slansky, incidentally, has been purged by the party, and is at this writing under arrest.

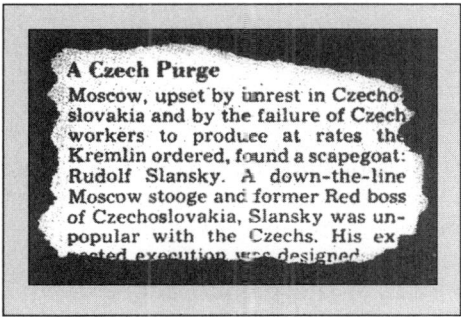

The excerpt to the left is taken from page 10 of the Dec. 10th QUICK magazine. Notice that although Slansky is identified as the "former Red Boss" of Czechoslovakia, he is not identified is a Jew.

JEWS IN AMERICA

Jewish historians divide Jewish immigration into the U. S. into three phases: the Sephardic or Spanish Period, the German Period and the Russian-Polish Period.

Sephardic Period

Since colonial America was still a pioneer country, there were almost no Jews here before the American Revolution. In 1776 there were certainly no more than a few score of Sephardic Jews in the entire country. Modern Jewish historians have tried to prove the existence of two Jewish privates in Washington's armies, but the question is of no consequence either way. By 1830—50 years after the Declaration of Independence, and 220 years after the founding of Jamestown—there were an estimated 10,000 Jews in the U.S., comprising perhaps 1/5th of 1% of the total population.

German Period

During this period a fairly steady trickle of German Jews came to the U.S. mainly from Germany, so that by 1880 they numbered about 250,000, out of a total population of 50 million—about 1/2 of 1%.

Russian-Polish Period

Following the assassination of Tsar Alexander II in 1881, vast numbers of Russian Jews inundated our port cities; between 1881 and 1917 our Jewish population increased by 1200%— to more than three millions!

World War I and the Russian Revolution added to this influx. Many Jews left Poland when as a result of the Versailles Treaty, it was made independent of Soviet Russia; others fled Russia during the counter-revolution and civil war which raged in 1918-1919-1920. The White Russian Armies, regarding Bolshevism as a Jewish movement, showed little mercy to those Jewish communities falling into their hands. Many Jews, fleeing these anti-communist armies, eventually made their way to the U.S.

This flood of immigration continued until 1924, when the Johnson-Lodge bill temporarily brought it to a halt. However, when the Roosevelt administration came to power in 1932, the barriers were once again lowered, so that in the calendar years of 1939, 52.3% of all immigrants admitted to the U.S. were Jewish. Since World War II this influx has continued under so-called DP legislation, with the result that approximately half of the world's Jewish population has now congregated here. Today, official Jewish sources estimate America's Jewish population to be (1949) 5,185,000. The actual figure is almost certainly higher, and may exceed 7 million...

NEW YORK: Jew Capital of the World

"The newly arrived Jews settled in the metropolitan centers, New York alone absorbing approximately half of the total Jewish immigration. But the "ghettoization" of the East-European Jews in the United States was the result not of objective forces only: it was as much the result of the immigrant's desire to retain all they could of their old way of life"—Page 218, The Jewish People, Past and Present, Central Yiddish Culture Organization (CYCO) New York.

New York City, with its more than two million Jews, has been the staging ground for the Jewish invasion of the U.S. Here the Jewish immigrant has found a ghetto-like environment similar to the one he left in east-Europe. Here he learns the language and customs of the country. Here he gathers know-how and capital before faring forth into the hinterland of America Soon he will be buying up a business on the Main Street of Los Angeles, or Dallas, or Chicago.

Many lower class Jews, being unable to learn the language or raise the capital, or being otherwise unequipped to go into business or the professions, have settled in New York to become workers and craftsmen. Thus we find Ben Gold's communistic fur workers union, and David Dubinsky's "socialistic" garment workers union, consisting almost entirely of Jews. As would be expected therefore New York City has been the seed-bed for communism in the United States.

U.S. Communist Party

The American Communist Party has never been very large in 1940 it had an estimated 80,000 members; it has perhaps half that many now. On first appearances this would seem to rule it out as a significant force in American politics. But appearances can be deceptive. Unlike the mass-recruited communist parties of France and Italy, the American communist party is small, carefully chosen, well disciplined, and fanatical. Few—perhaps no one—of its membership has been recruited from the sweaty-shirt strata. its members are college professors and union leaders, physicists and government workers, reporters, playrights and business executives, actors and newspaper reporters. Some of its members are wealthy; almost all are well educated. Its chief asset is its ability to mobilize the combined forces of American Jewry to its use.

THE TREASON TRIALS

Since early 1945 the communist party has been involved, in

a series of highly publicized treason and conspiracy trials utterly without precedent in American history These included the "Amerasia Case," the "Gerhart Eisler Case," the "Judith Coplin Case," the "Alger Hiss Case," the "Hollywood Ten Case," the "Fuchs-Gold Atom Spy Case," the "Rosenberg-Sobell Case," and the case of "Eugene Dennis and the Convicted Eleven."

It was impossible, of course, to conceal altogether the Jewishness of the overwhelming majority of the defendants. But Jewish propagandists exhausted every trick in trying. One Jewish publication—Look magazine—ran a picture story on the spy trials in which the defendants were variously described as "typical Americans"... "American born" . . and "as American as apple pie." So there will be no further doubt regarding the racial identity of the American communist party, we have accumulated photographs and data on virtually every communist indicted or tried for communistic activity since 1945. The reader may judge for himself.

AMERASIA CASE

In early 1945 the FBI arrested six individuals, three of whom are known Jews, for stealing 1700 highly confidential documents from State Department files. This was the Amerasia Case. Those arrested were:

PHILIP JAFFE, a Russian Jew who came to the U.S. in 1905. He was editor of the magazine, "Amerasia," and was the former editor of the communist paper, "Labor Defense." He was convicted and fined.

ANDREW ROTH, a Brooklyn born Jew with

Philip Jaffe, editor of "Amerasia," and head of the ring which stole 1700 secret documents. Like many other high ranking reds, he originally came from the Pale of Settlement.

a lieutenant's commission in Naval Intelligence.

MARK GAYN, a writer, born in Manchuria of Russian-Jewish parents. His Jew name is Julius Ginsberg.

JOHN STEWART SERVICE, a high State Department official who gave Jaffe much of the stolen material He is believed to be a gentile

ALSO ARRESTED were Emmanuel Larsen and Kate Mitchel, nationality unknown.

Only two of those arrested were actually brought to trial, although the Justice Department's case was considered airtight. The trial of the ringleader, Philip Jaffe, was one of the strangest on record. Late one Friday afternoon he was rushed into court without any previous notice or publicity, and before anyone knew what was going on he pleaded guilty, and was sentenced and finec By paying the comparatively insignificant sum of $1,500.00 he was relieved from the danger of any future prosecution. Roth paid a $500.00 fine.

John Stewart Service was not prosecuted, nor was he discharged from his high State Department position. The State Department, despite the constant prodding of Senator McCarthy of Wisconsin, refused to accept the evidence against him. Four times he was called before the State Department's "loyalty board," and four times he was cleared.

Andrew Roth aided in the theft of State Department documents. He is a Brooklyn Jew.

John Stewart Service

This in spite of an FBI wire recording of his transactions with Jaffe! Not until the fifth loyalty hearing was it decided that there were "reasonable" grounds for suspecting his loyalty. This came six years after the original arrests. Somewhere, hidden hands were pulling wires...

ALGER HISS CASE

The second treason case also involved the State Department. This was the trial of Alger Hiss, protege of Supreme Court Justice Felix Frankfurter. Hiss, like Acheson, was a student under Frankfurter at Harvard.

Hiss was one of the most influential men in the State Department. At Yalta he had been a Roosevelt advisor; at San Francisco he helped draw up the United Nations charter. And he was an intimate friend of the secretary-of-state.

Hiss, although a communist, was not convicted for being one. He perjured himself by denying his communist activities, however, and it was on this charge that he was tried and convicted.

The Alger Hiss trial was also a unique one. Dean Acheson's wife campaigned to raise funds for his defense. Acheson himself declared: "I'll not turn my back on Alger Hiss." Felix Frankfurter actually took the witness stand to testify as a character witness for his protege. In spite of all this, Hiss was convicted and sent to the penitentiary.

Frankfurter's role in this treasonable drama is worth commenting on. An immigrant Jew from Austria, he has a life-long affinity for pro-Marxist causes. He first attained prominence as one of the defenders of Sacco and Vanzetti.

Frankfurter, along with Lehman and Henry Morgantheau, is one of the most influential Jews in America today. In addition to Acheson and Hiss, he has been responsible for the placing of an estimated 200 of his "proteges" in high places. These include: (1) Nathan Witt, former general secretary of the National Labor Relations Board; (2) Lee Pressman, chief legal counsel for the CIO; (3) John Abt, key attorney for the SEC, AAA, and WPA. All are Marxist Jews; Pressman has admitted being a card carrying party member.

Frankfurter may or may not be a communist, but an amazing number of his proteges, including Alger Hiss, have turned out to be. That was the background of the Alger Hiss Case.

Judith Coplin

One of the most publicized treason trials was that of Jewish Judith Coplin in June of 1949. She was caught red-handed passing classified documents from Justice Department files to a Russian agent, who happened to be employed by the United Nations. She was convicted of espionage and sentenced to 15 years in prison. Later the conviction was set aside by the Supreme Court on the grounds that the FBI had arrested her improperly and without a warrant. It pays to have a friend on the Supreme Court, or so it would seem...

Judith Coplin, a convicted spy, is also Jewish. She worked for the Justice Department.

Gerhart Eisler, highest ranking communist ever convicted in the U.S. He's Jewish.

Gerhart Eisler

The highest ranking communist ever brought to trial in the U.S. was Gerhart Eisler. Between 1935 and February of 1947 he was the secret boss of the Communist Party in the U.S. In those years he commuted regularly between the U.S. and Russia, using the aliases Berger, Brown, Edwards, and others. His right hand man, and the second ranking cominform agent in the U.S. was J. Peters, author of the "Peters Manuel." His real name was Goldberger, and like Eisler he is Jewish.

Several of Eisler's family have also been prominent in the Party. A brother, Hans, has built an outstanding reputation as a writer of revolutionary songs. He is presently employed as a songwriter in Hollywood. A sister, Ruth Fischer, was a communist agent for a number of years.

In May of 1950, while free on bail, Eisler fled the U.S. on the Polish ship Batory and is now propaganda chief of Russian-occupied Eastern Germany.

The Hollywood Ten

In 1950 the ten leading film writers of the Hollywood Film Colony, nine of whom are known Jews, were convicted for contempt of Congress and sentenced to prison. All had appeared before the House Committee on Un-American Activities in 1948, and all had refused to testify.

The Film Colony went all-out in its support. A group of film notables, including Lauren Bacall and Humphrey Bogart, chartered a special plane to Washington. Jewish publications everywhere raised the cry that the Un-American Activities Committee was victimizing a group of artists who, at the worst, were liberally inclined.

Shown above are the convicted "Hollywood Ten." All wear $200.00 suits, all are in the one-to-five thousand dollar a week income bracket. All of them are Yiddish except one.

As events proved, the committee knew exactly what it was doing. Six of the "Hollywood Ten" were communist party members. The other four had flagrantly pro-communist records. Furthermore, as screen writers they were in a particularly advantageous position to insert subtle bits of red propaganda into pictures. Given here is a roll-call of the Hollywood Ten:

(1) Alvah Bessie, a screen-writer. A communist party member, he wrote for the party publication, New Masses.

(2) Herbert Biberman, received a six month sentence and a $l,000.00 fine. A party member, he is the Yiddish husband of academy award winning actress Gale Sondergaard.

(3) Lester Cole, also a party member.

(4) Edward Dmytryk, who belongs to 15 fronts. Fined and sentenced.

(5) Ring Lardner, Jr., a script writer and party member.

(6) John Howard Lawson, a Broadway playwright and screen writer. Wrote "Professional," "Success Story." A party member.

(7) Albert Maltz, wrote "Merry-go-Round," "Snake Pit." A party member.

(8) Sam Ornitz, a screen writer.

(9) Adrian Scott, nationality not verified.

(10) Dalton Trumbo, a party member.

The American Politburo

One of the top news stories of 1949 was the trial of Eugene Dennis and the Convicted Eleven. Collectively, this group comprised the National Secretariat of the American Communist Party; in other words, the American Politburo.

The much publicized trial was held in the court of Judge Harold Medina. Perhaps no other single event has served better to demonstrate the Jewishness of the American communist party. Here were the top party executives driven out into the open for everybody to see. How many were Jewish? At least six. They are:

(1) Jacob Stachel, a Russian-born Jew and still an alien.

(2) John Gates (Jew name Israel Regenstreif), editor-

The "Convicted Eleven" were, next to Gerhart Eisler, the highest ranking communists ever convicted in the U.S. This "American Politburo" consisted of six Jews and five non-Jews.

in-chief of the Daily Worker and a former officer in the Communist Brigade in Spain.

(3) Gilbert Green (Greenberg).

(4) Gus Hall (Jew name, Arvo Mike Haeberg), son of Lithuanian-Jewish parents.

(5) Irving Potash, a Russian-born Jew.

(6) Carl Winter (Jew name Philip Carl Weissberg).

The racial identity of Eugene Dennis (Waldron), Robert Thompson, and John Williamson has not been determined.

Ten of the eleven were sentenced to 5 years in federal prison and fined $10,000.00 each. Thompson received a three year sentence.

The Fuchs-Gold Spy Ring

On February 3rd, 1949, British intelligence agents arrested a diminutive German-born atomic scientist by the name of Klaus Fuchs. He was accused, and subsequently convicted, of passing atomic secrets to the Russians.

Klaus Fuchs

At the beginning of World War II Fuchs had been interned by the British as an enemy alien. He was subsequently released from British custody and admitted to the U.S. at the personal instigation of Albert Einstein. As a scientist for the Manhattan Project, he had access to our innermost atomic secrets between 1942 and 1945, and he is said to be one of the few men familiar with the overall construction of the A-bomb. He is now serving a penitentiary term in England for espionage.

Acting on information obtained from Fuchs, the FBI began a series of investigations which resulted in the eventual arrest of nine other members of the ring. Of these nine, all of whom were later convicted, eight were Jewish. Here is a brief description of the entire ring:

Harry Gold (Jew name Goldodnitsky). A chemist, he was born in Switzerland of Russian-Jewish parents. He studied at Drexel University, University of Pennsylvania, and Xavier University He was a courier for the Soviet espionage chief, S. M. Semenov, who used the Amtorg Trading Corporation as a base of operations. Gold travelled all over the country collecting information from ring members strategically placed in defense and atomic energy installations. Arrested in May of 1950, he pleaded guilty of espionage and received 30 years in prison.

Harry Gold

David Greenglass

David Greenglass, the son of a Russian-Jewish father and a Polish-Jewish mother, was one of those who passed atomic information to Gold. Between 1943 and 1946 he was employed at the vital atomic installation at Los Alamos, New Mexico. He also gave Julius Rosenberg vital information concerning the "fuse" used to detonate the A-bomb. Significantly, the chief of the Los Alamos project

Abraham Brothman

Robert Oppenheimer

Israel Weinbaum

Miriam Moscowitz

at this time was the Jew, Robt. Oppenheimer. Klaus Fuchs was also passing A-bomb information to Harry Gold from Los Alamos during this period.

Abraham Brothman was another member of the ring. He headed the engineering firm of A. Brothman and Associates, Long Island, N. Y. He supplied Gold with secret data on aviation gasoline, turbo aircraft engines, and synthetic rubber. So valuable was his contribution that a Russian official allegedly told him his efforts were worth two brigades to Soviet Russia. He was arrested on July 27th, 1950, for conspiracy against the U.S. and was convicted.

Miriam Moskowitz was also caught in the spy net. A graduate of the City College of NYC, she was arrested August 17, 1950 as part of the same apparatus. She was employed by the War Manpower Commission between 1942-44, and was later associated with the Brothman firm. Miriam is Yiddish. She was convicted.

Sidney Weinbaum, a product of Russia's "Charkoff" Institute of Technology, came to the U.S. in 1922. His real name is Israel Weinbaum. He was connected with the radiation laboratory at CalTech for four years, during which time he furnished the Soviet government with atomic secrets. He was convicted on a perjury charge.

Alfred Dean Slack, was the only gentile besides Fuchs to be apprehended. While employed at the Oak

Ridge establishment he gave atomic information to Harry Gold. He is also believed to have given Gold intelligence about a new secret explosive while employed at the Holtson Ordnance Works at Kingsport, Tenn. His alma mater is Syracuse University.

The Rosenbergs

Three other members of the Fuchs-Gold ring were also arrested. However, unlike the first seven—who pleaded guilty—they chose to plead "not guilty." As a result two of them—Julius and Ethel Rosenberg—received the death penalty and the third, Morton Sobell, received 30 years in prison.

Julius Rosenberg was born of Russian-Jewish parents. An electrical engineer and a graduate of the City College of New York City, he was instrumental in recruiting Greenglass into the spy ring. While employed at the Emerson Electric Company he stole the plans for the highly secret proximity fuse which is now being used against American planes in Korea. He also aided in the theft of atomic secrets: His job was to digest information from Greenglass, and then pass it on to Soviet agents. He was sentenced to death.

Ethel Rosenberg, wife of Julius, was convicted of the

Morton Sobell

Julius and Ethel Rosenberg

same charges at the same time. She is a sister of David Greenglass. David Greenglass's wife acted as a courier between Greenglass and the Rosenbergs, but for some reason was not put on trial.

Morton Sobell was also a graduate of the City College of New York City. He and Rosenberg were classmates together. Sobell passed electronic data to Rosenberg, including radar secrets. He fled to Mexico to escape arrest, was returned by Mexican authorities. He was convicted for conspiracy to commit espionage and was sentenced to 30 years in prison.

Behind the Atom Treason

The question which instantly comes to mind is: how were communist agents able to ferret out our valuable atom secrets when so much secrecy surrounded the entire project? Why was it that Russia had the full secret of atom-bomb manufacture before the American people even knew of the existence of atomic weapons? These questions are especially puzzling when we consider the fantastic security measures taken to safeguard the secret. Bob Considine once described a fire which burned down a large building housing an atomic installation. Although firemen could have easily saved the building, plant guards would not permit them to enter the restricted area because they didn't have authorized passes! Not even members of the U.S. Congress were let in on the secret. Yet the Soviet agents were able to penetrate this security wall as though it weren't there. How did they do it?

First it should be remembered that a central figure in the atomic program was Albert Einstein, a foreign-born Jew with a record of 16 red fronts to his credit. It has never been proven that Einstein is an actual party member, but there can be absolutely no doubt as to where his sympathies lie. Nor can there be any doubt regarding the red tint of his friends. A list of those around Einstein reads like a Who's Who of Communism. It was Einstein who was instrumental in having Fuchs brought to the United States.

Furthermore, it should be remembered that the chief of the Los Alamos installation between 1943-45, when most of the secrets were stolen, was the Jew, Robert Oppenheimer. Robert Oppenheimer has a brother, Frank, who is also an atomic scientist and who is, or was, a card carrying

Left to right: W. W. Waymack, L. L. Straus*, David Lilienthal*, R. F. Bacher*, Sumner Pike. In 1945 Harry Truman removed atomic energy from military authority and placed it under this Jew-dominated board, headed by David Lilienthal. Lilienthal had a pro-communist record.

communist. Frank Oppenheimer belonged to "Professional Unit No. 122 of the Communist Party," while on the staff at Cal-Tech.

Finally, it should be noted that shortly after V-J day Harry Truman turned America's atomic energy program over to a board consisting of five men, three of whom were Jews. Not only that, but the Jewish chairman, David Lilienthal, had belonged to at least two communist fronts previous to his appointment. This was the background to the atom treason.

Left to right: W. W. Waymack, L. L. Straus*, David Lilienthal*, R. F. Bacher*, Sumner Pike. In 1945 Harry Truman removed atomic energy from military authority and placed it under this Jew-dominated board, headed by David Lilienthal. Lilienthal had a pro-communist record.

Scientist X

There have been other instances of Jewish treason in our atomic energy program. Witness the case of the much publicized "Scientist X" who from 1943 on passed vital atomic information to Steve Nelson.

"Scientist X" proved to be a Jew by the name of Joseph W. Weinberg of the University of Minnesota.

Steve Nelson

Steve Nelson? His real name is Mesarosh and his birthplace is Belgrade. "Nelson" studied at the Lenin Institute in Moscow and resided in Russia from September of 1931 to July 1943. Recently cited for contempt of Congress, he was originally arrested for deportation in 1922 when it was found that he had fraudulently entered this country by using the passport of one Joseph Fleishinger, a cousin...

Canadian Spy Ring

Canada has also had spy trouble. There as in the U.S. the Soviet Embassy served as headquarters for espionage activity. There, as in the U.S. the principal characters in the plot were Jews.

In early 1945 an employee of the Russian embassy in Ottawa packed hundreds of secret Russian documents into a suitcase and turned himself over to Canadian authorities. As a result, a spy ring was uncovered which included—among others—a member of the Canadian Parliament and a professor at McGill university. Leader of the ring, and by far its most important member, was Fred Rose (Rosenberg) the only communist in the Canadian Parliament. Rose, a Polish-Jew. was the ringleader, the recruiter, and the courier for the ring.

Fred Rose, member of Parliament and leader of the Canadian Spy Ring, is a Polish-Jew

On June 16, 1946, he was sentenced to prison for his activities. The following year (Dec. 6. 1947) Dr. Raymond Boyer, a professor at McGill university was sentenced to two years in prison for having given Rose information concerning the secret explosive, RDX. Boyer was married to the Jewess, Anita Cohen. Arraigned with Rose were Samuel Gerson (of Russian-Jewish parentage), and David Shugar, believed to be Jewish. Other Jews implicated in the Fred Rose spy ring included: J. Isidor Gottheil, Israel Halperin, and Sam Carr (Cohen). (NOTE: This is not a complete listing of the Fred Rose spy ring.)

Second-String Politburo

Soon after the conviction of the Eugene Dennis crew, a second-string politburo was scheduled to assume control of the party apparatus. This new politburo consisted of 21 members, 14 of whom are Jewish. On June 21, 1951, the Justice Department indicted the entire group for conspiracy against the United States government. At the present writing they are free on bail pending trial. Here is the roll-call:

(1) Israel Amter, 70, a long-time party stalwart. He organized the "Friends of the Soviet Union in the U.S.," a front

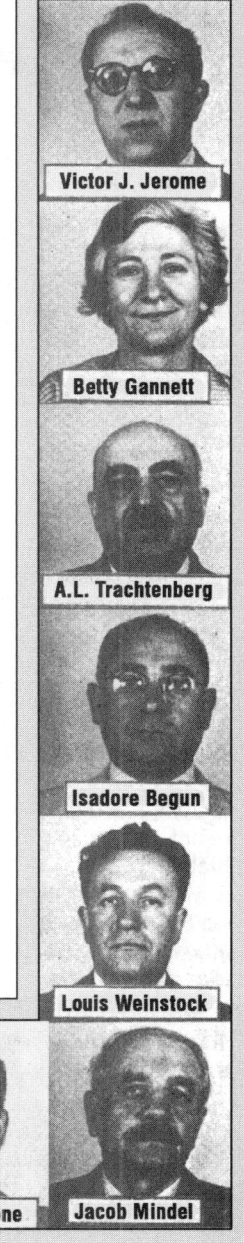

George B Charney
Simon Gerson
Albert F. Lannon
Elizabeth G. Flynn
Claudia Jones
Pettis Perry

organization which numbers Albert Einstein among its prominent members.

(2) Marian Maxwell Abt, 52, public relations director and secretary of the party's "Defense Commission." She is a Chicago Jewess.

(3) Isidore Begun, 47, a Russian-Jew who formerly taught in New York City's public schools. He is a party writer and lecturer.

(4) Alexander Bittelman, 61, a Russian-Jew, and reputed to be "one of the foremost theoreticians and dialecticians of the party."

(5) George B. Charney, 46, a Russian-Jew. He is the trade union secretary of the N. Y. state communist party.

(6) Elizabeth Gurley Flynn, 60, chairman of the party's "Women's Commission." A gentile, she was born in Concord, N. H.

(7) Betty Gannett, 44, national education director for the party. She is a Polish-Jewess, and still an alien.

(8) Simon W. Gerson, 41, chairman of the party's "N. Y. State Legislative Bureau." He is believed to be Jewish.

(9) Victory Jeremy Jerome, 54, chairman of the party's cultural commission. He is a Polish-Jew.

(10) Arnold Samuel Johnson, temporary chairman of District 5 Western Pennsylvania. Born in Seattle, he is a gentile

(11) Claudia Jones, 36, secretary of the party's "National Women's Commission." She is a Trinidad Negress and an alien.

(12) Albert Francis Lannon, 43, party's "National Maritime Coordinator" and president of the "Communist Political

Association of Maryland and Washington, D. C." Nationality unknown.

(13) Jacob Mindel, 69, an old-time party wheelhorse. He is a Russian Jew.

(14) Petty Perres, 54, national secretary of the party's Negro Commission.

(15) Alexander Trachtenberg, head of International Publishers, Inc.

(16) Louis Weinstock, 48, member of the party's "National Review Commission." He is a Hungarian Jew.

(17) Wm. Wold Weinstone, 53, a charter member of the party and a former secretary of its Michigan branch. A Russian-Jew.

(18) Fred Fine, 37, secretary of the party's "Public Affairs Commission." He is a Chicago Jew.

(19) James Edward Jackson, 36, the party's "Southern Regional Director." He is colored.

(20) Wm. Norman Marron, 49, executive secretary of the N. Y. State Communist Party. He is a Russian-Jew.

(21) Sidney Steinberg, the party's "Assistant National Labor Secretary." He is a Lithuanian Jew.

THE ROUNDUP

On July 26th, 1951, the FBI arrested the 15 leading communist party officials on the West Coast (see preceding page). They were all identified by the FBI as second-string leaders, the top leadership being already under detention. A few days later, on August 7th, five second-string leaders were also arrested in the east. All were charged with conspiracy to overthrow the U.S. government.

Of the 15 arrested on the West Coast, six have been identified as Jews. They are

The Roundup: Left to right: Steinberg, Kusnitz, Healey, Connelly. Four of the fifteen reds rounded up on the West Coast are shown above. While the top leaders of the party is almost totally Yiddish, the lower echelons contain many gentiles, who fill minor executive positions.

The Roundup: Left to right: Roy Wood, Regina Frankfeld, George Meyers, Philip Frankfeld, Rose Blumberg.

(1) Henry Steinberg, a Polish-Jew; (2) Rose Chernin (Kusnitz), a Russian-Jewess; (3) Frank Carlson, a Russian Jew; (4) Ben Dobbs, a New York Jew; (5) Frank Spector, a Russian-Jew; (6) Al Richmond, a Russian Jew. Of the remaining nine, Dorothy Healey, Philip Connelly, and Otto Fox are gentile; Carl Rude Lambert is believed to be Jewish, and the identity of the others has not been determined.

Of the five arrested in the east, four are Jewish. They are: (1) Roy Wood, 36, a gentile and chairman of the Washington D.C., Communist Party; (2) Regina Frankfeld, 41, a party organizer in Cleveland; (3) George Meyers, 38, a party organizer; (4) Philip Frankfield, 44, an organizer; (5) Rose Blumberg, of Brooklyn. All except Wood are Yiddish.

THREE GENTILES

Perhaps some attention should be devoted to three gentiles who have figured prominently in several of the treason trials, and whose names have constantly appeared in the press for several years. The three are:

Whittaker Chambers, Elizabeth Bentley, and Vanderbilt Field.

None of the three has been indicted nor convicted of a crime, and none at the present time are party members. In fact, two have become enemies of Communism. Nevertheless they deserve a place in any description of the American communist party.

Vanderbilt Field

Because he is a gentile and because he has a famous name, Vanderbilt Field is perhaps better known to the American public than any other member of the communist conspiracy. This prominence is not accidental. Jewish propagandists, whether communist or not, invariably seek to conceal the Jewish nature of Communism by giving lavish publicity to gentiles such as Field. As a point of fact, Field does not belong to party, nor was he among those arrested when the top leadership was being rounded up.

Field is secretary of the "Civil Rights Congress Bail Fund," which is intrusted with raising bail for party members in trouble. He is married to the Jewess, Anita Cohen, former

Vanderbilt Field (above right) is secretary of the so-called "Civil Rights Committee," which provides bail-bond for convicted Reds. He is shown leaving the courtroom after being questioned regarding the source of the Committee's funds. Accompanying him are his Jewish lawyer and two other members of the "Civil Rights Committee."

wife of the convicted spy, Raymond Boyer.

Whittaker Chambers

One of the principal witnesses against Alger Hiss at his trial was Whittaker Chambers, who like Hiss is a gentile. Chambers—of pumpkin letter fame—was formerly an editor of the Daily Worker and later an associate editor of Time magazine. A product of Columbia university Chambers began his underground work for the party in 1932. He has since renounced communism and has joined the Catholic Church. Like Elizabeth Bentley, he has given invaluable aid to the FBI and the un-American activities committee in their efforts to track down key members of the communist party. Chambers is married to a Jewess.

Whittaker Chambers

Elizabeth Bentley

Elizabeth Bentley, a product of Vassar, is another former communist who has done much to expose the communist underground. For several years she served as a courier for a communist espionage network. She was the mistress of the Jew, Jacob Golos, a trusted Soviet agent and her immediate superior. He died of a heart attack on Thanksgiving day, 1943. It was after his death that Elizabeth Bentley turned against the party. Since then she has co-operated with the FBI and the un-American Activities Committee.

Elizabeth Bentley

COMMUNISM IN HOLLYWOOD

No discussion of communism would be complete without giving some attention to the Hollywood scene. Within the

Jacob Golos

past few years a number of investigations by the House Committee on Un-American Activities, and by California's "Tenney Committee," have unearthed a veritable hotbed of Communism in the movie colony. We have already made some mention of the convicted "Hollywood Ten" who received sentences for contempt of congress. There are literally hundreds of other high placed Jews with pro-communist records in the film colony, including millionaire actors, directors, producers, writers, and executives.

The question immediately arises as to why so many of these wealthy and privileged Jews embrace Communism. The answer is, of course, that communism is not an economic movement, but a racial movement. Communism cannot be understood, or dealt with, on any other basis.

An Easy Target

There is a question in the minds of many as to how and why the Communists took over Hollywood. To begin with, the Hollywood motion picture industry is the most important vehicle of propaganda in the English speaking world today. In the long run Hollywood exerts a greater influence over the English speaking peoples than all other propaganda mediums combined. It has therefore become a prime target for communist infiltration. And since the film industry is overwhelmingly Jewish, communist agents encountered a minimum of difficulty in setting up shop. To give the reader some idea as to the extent of the Jewish control over Hollywood, we have prepared the following survey of the motion picture industry

Jews Own the Film Industry

The Hollywood film industry is almost exclusively a Jewish enterprise. In the entire industry there are two, and only two, major Hollywood film producers operated by gentiles. All the rest are Jew-owned.

The two gentile firms are Twentieth-Century Fox, and RKO Pictures. Both companies, it should be noted, were

Among the motion picture executives, the following are Jewish: Harry Warner, Louis B. Mayer, Dore Schary, Joseph Schenck, Samuel Goldwyn, Barney Balaban, Nate J. Blumberg, Irving Briskin, Emmanuel Cohn, Harry Cohn, Armand Deutch, Robert Lippert, Marcus Loew, Simon S. Sylvan, Leo Spitz, Adolph Zukor. There are scores of others. Since 90% of the executives are Yiddish, it might be simpler to list the gentile ones.

Jews not only own the industry, but they fill the key position as well. Among the Jewish producers and dirctors are the following: Ben Hecht, Garson Kanin, Elia Kazan, Norman Krasna, Mervyn LeRoy (married a Jewess), Artur Lubin, David Selznick, Jerry Wald, Walter Wanger, Norman Taurog, Bert Friedlob, Michael Curtiz, Max Fleischer, Pandro S. Berman, Michael Balcon, William Goetz, Joseph Pasternack, Herman Mankiewicz, Ernest Lubitch, Sol Siegel, William Wellman, Sam Zimbalist, Samuel J. Briskin, George Cukor, Irving Cummings, Leo Forbstein, William Fox, Marion Gering, Albert Kaufman, Alexander Korda (Br.), Carl Laemmie, Sidney Lanfield, Mitchell Leisen, Sol Lesser, Harry Rapf, Irving Rapper, Max Reinhardt, Charles Rogers, Mark R. Sandrich, Alfred Santel, I.J. Schnitzer, Jack H. Skirball, John N. Stahl, Joseph von Sternberg.

originally formed by Jews, and were Jew owned and operated until recently. In 1948 Howard Hughes bought an eight million dollar bloc of RKO stock (assets of the firm are $113,638,000.00) and since then has been prominent in directing its affairs. The other gentile firm is 20th Century Fox, whose president is Spyros Skouras, a Greek.

The Big Three

The three largest motion picture firms in Hollywood are completely Jewish, and in a very real sense they dominate the industry. The "Big Three" are:

LOEWS, INC., the giant of the industry, with assets listed at $223,141,585.43. Its founder was Marcus Loew, a Jew, and its current president is Nicholas Schenck, a Russian-Jew from the Pale of Settlement. Loews, Inc. owns Metro-Goldwyn-Mayer (MGM), whose president was Louis B. Mayer for many years. Dore Schary, a Jew with four communist

> Note: The following Jewish writers are prominent. (*indicates communist front affiliation). Norman Corwin, Oscar Hammerstein II*, Moss Hart*, Lorenzo Hart, Lillian Hellman*, Fannie Hurst, George S. Kaufman*, Sidney Kingsley, John Howard Lawson*, Edward Dmytryk*, Alvah Bessie*, Lester Cole*, Ring Lardner Jr.*, John Howard Lawson*, Albert Maltz*, Sam Ornitz*, Dalton Trumbo*, Clifford Odets*, Dorothy Parker*, Elmer Rice*, Richard Rodgers, Irwin Shaw*, George Sklar*, Sam Spewack, John Wexley*, Morrie Ryskind, Richard Maibaum, Edwin Justis Mayer*, Arthur Sheekman, Leonardo Bercovici*, Allen Boretz, Sidney Buchman*, Edward Chodorov*, Jerome Chodorov*, Howard Dietz, Julius Epstein*, Philip Epstein*, Dorothy Fields, Herbert Fields, Joseph Fields, Daniel Fuchs, Michael Gold*, Edmund Goulding, Howard J. Green, Sam Hellman, S.G. Hoffenstein, James Rian, Arthur Kober*. Perhaps the reader will understand how communist propaganda gets into the movies after seeing this partial list of pro-communist writers employed by the film companies.

fronts to his credit, now heads MGM.

PARAMOUNT PICTURES, INC., with assets listed at $185,588,505.00, is the second largest film producer in Hollywood. Its president is the Jew, Barney Balaban. Paramount also owns the American Broadcasting Company (ABC).

WARNER BROTHERS PICTURES, INC., is the third largest picture company in Hollywood, with assets of $176,284,761.00. Its president is Harry Warner, a Polish Jew. There were originally four Warner brothers: Samuel, Harry, Albert, and Jack. In addition to their Hollywood holdings, the brothers at one time owned 530 theatres in the U.S., and 35 film exchanges throughout the world.

Positions number four and five go to 20th Century Fox and RKO Pictures, described above.

UNIVERSAL PICTURES, INC., with assets of $47,984,034.00 is the sixth largest film company in Hollywood. Its president is the Jew, Nate J. Blumberg.

COLUMBIA PICTURES, INC., with assets of $39,521,240.00, is number seven in Hollywood. Its president is the New York Jew, Harry Cohn.

This completes the roster of Hollywood picture producers with assets of twenty million dollars or more. Of the seven firms listed above, five are totally Jewish owned and operated, and the other two were formerly Jewish owned, and may still be in part. There are several smaller firms which we have not listed, and they too are overwhelmingly Jewish. (Note: Above names and figures apply to the year 1950)

"Kosher Valley"

Hollywood has become a Jew town. The Fairfax area, which is the heart of the Hollywood residential district, is slightly more than 60% Jewish, according to Jewish statistics

Because the Hollywood stars are the industry's stock-in-trade—its merchandise, so to speak—they are mostly gentile. A given picture may have a Jew producer, a Jew director, and Jew writer, but generally all the public sees is the prettied-up gentile actor. But even this generalization is breaking down to a surprising degree. An amazing number of actors (and almost all the bit players and extras) are either Jewish, or married to Jews. In Hollywood many a blond Christian girl has found her way to stardom by marrying (or going to bed with) a hook-nosed Khazar Jew. Here is a partial list of Hollywood stars who are, or have been, married to Jews: Doris Day (Melcher), Lili Palmer (Peiser), Janet Leigh (Curtis-Schwartz), Claudette Colbert (Pressman), Anita Louise (Adler), Madge Evans (Kingsley), Jennifer Jones (Selznick), Joan Bennett (Wanger), Alan Ladd (Carol-Lederer), Merle Oberon (Korda), Joyce Matthews (Berle), Eleanor Parker (Friedlob), Norma Shearer (Thalberg), Ruth Roman (Hall-Schiff), Nancy Olson (Lerner), Eleanor Holms (Rose), Gig Young (Rosenstein), Miriam Hopkins (Litvak), Myrna Dell (Buchtel), Wendy Barrie (Meyer), Jean Howard (Feldman), Joan Blair (Coplin), Dick Powell (Blondell), Gary Merrill (Jolson), John Loder (Lamar), Gale Sondergaard (Biberman), Norma Talmadge (Schenck). There are many, many others.

Jennifer Jones

Ruth Roman

> Hollywood is in more ways than one the land of make-believe. The film industry can take a pock-marked, flat-chested little Jewess out of the ghettoes of Poland and make her into a glamour girl, envied and aped by millions. They straighten her nose, pull her teeth, bleach her hair, give her a new complexion with make-up putty, paint on new lips, pad her bust and hips, and adjust the microphones to give her a pleasing voice. A million dollar publicity campaign does the rest. Frequently that is the formula by which a Jew-star is born.
>
>
> Danny Kaye
>
> Here is a partial list of Hollywood's Jew-stars (*indicates communist front affiliation.): Eddie Cantor*, Binnie Barnes (Gittel), Joan Blondell, Charlie Chaplin* (Thonstein), Tony Curtis (Schwartz), Bette Davis*, Marlene Dietrich, Melvyn Douglas* (Hesselberg), Deanna Durbin, John Garfield* (Garfinkle), Frankie Laine, Hedy Lamarr (Keisler), Paulette Goddard*, Douglas Fairbanks* (Ullman), Judy Garland (Gumm), Judy Holiday* (Tuvim), Paul Muni (Weisenfreund), Danny Kaye* (Kaminsky), Larry Parks*, Groucho Marx*, Martha Raye, Edward G. Robinson* (Goldenberg), Kennan Wynn* (Leopold), Ed Wynn, Farley Granger, Sylvia Sidney* (Koskow), Robert Merrill, The Ritz Brothers, The Andrews Sisters, Henry Morgan*, Bobby Breen, Benny Baker* (Zifkin), Jack Benny (Kubelsky), Mary Livingston (Marks), George Burns (Birnbaum), Gracie Allen, Theda Bari (Goodman), J Edward Bromberg* (Bromberger), Kitty Carlisle, Sue Carol (Lederer), Ricardo Cortez, Milton Berle, Sally Eilers, Mary Ellis, Al Jolson, Bert Lahr, Francis Lederer, Lew Lehr, Jerry Lewis, Peter Lorre, Alice McMahon, Pola Negri, Parkyakarkas (Harry Einstein), Luise Ranier, Gregory Ratoff, Victor Borge, Pinkey Lee, Adolph Menjou, Mischa Auer. (In fairness, the last two names are violently anti-communist. Menjou is married to a Christian woman, Auer is converted to Christianity. Both have had difficulty in finding work because of their anti-communistic stand). Other Jew stars include: Sammy Kaye, Stella Adler, Morrie Amsterdam, Albert Basserman, Polly Bergen, Elizabeth Bergner, Morris Carnovsky, Mary Ellis, Sydney Fox, Sam Jaffe, Sam Levine, Noel Madison, Carmel Meyer, Maurice Mosovitch, Florence Reed, Joseph Schildkraut, Sid Silvers, George Stone, Conrad Veidt, Lous Wolheim. There are, of course, hundreds of others.

(published in the California Jewish Voice). Virtually every shop and store in Hollywood is Jew-owned. The Jews operate the theatres, restaurants, drug stores, clothing stores—even the cigarette machines. A visit to the neighborhood theatres and eating places will indicate even to the skeptic that Hollywood is predominately inhabited by east-European Jews. In nearby Los Angeles, Hollywood is sometimes referred to as "Kosher Valley"...

Propaganda in the Movies

For many years Hollywood limited its activities to the more subtle types of propaganda, but in recent years this has

> Hollywood is literally crawling with eastern European Jews who hold down high paying jobs in the film industry. Here is a miscellaneous list of high-paid Jews in Hollywood (*indicates communist front affiliation): Milton Sperling*, Irving Pichel*, Vincente Minnelli*, Anatole Litvak*, Benjamin Kahane, Dashiel Hammet*, William Gropper*, Lewis Browne, Larry Adler*, Harry Akst, Carlton Alsop, Leonard Berstein, Herman Bing, David Diamond, Charles Einfeld, Sylvia fine, H. Freulick, David Garber, Benjamin Glazer, Harry Green, Monroe Greenthal, Bernard Herzbrun, B.F. Holzman, S.G. Holzman, Samuel Keglin, George E. Kann, Sam Katz, Arthur R. Kohn, Jesse Lasky, Michael C. Levee, Sam Levene*, Ray Lissner, Emil Ludwig, Abe Polonsky*, Harold J. Rome*, Joseph Isaac Schnitzer, Edward Selzer, Milton Shumlin*, Harry Tobias, manny Wolf, Jack Yellen.
> The following are the leading musical directors in Hollywood: Nathanial Finston, Boris Morros, Erno Rapee, Max Steiner, Alfred Newman, Hugo Reisenfeld. The following Jewish musicians, although not strictly Hollywood personalities, are nevertheless indirectly associated with the film colony: Jascha Heifetz, Mischa Elman, Fritz Kreisler, Yehudi Menuhin, Nathan Milstein, Joseph Szegeti, Isaac Stern, Artur Schnabel, Oscar Levant, Artur Rubenstein, Vladimir Horowitz, Alexander Brailowsky, Wanda Landowski, Jan Peerce.

changed. Hollywood has now committed itself to producing at least four "race" pictures annually. Most of these pictures are destined beforehand to lose money, and are made for purely propaganda purposes. Some are so inflammatory they cannot be shown in certain sections of the United States.

Typical examples of this type of picture are: "Intruder in the Dust," "Pinky," "Crossfire," "Gentleman's Agreement," "No Way Out," and "Home of the Brave." Invariably these pictures seek to inflame minority groups by portraying them as being abused and persecuted by white "bigots." Such propaganda is frankly designed to arouse race hatred among Negroes, Mexicans, Jews, and other so-called minority groups. These people are being systematically taught to think and act in terms of race—they are being taught a hate philosophy. But there is another aspect to this kind of propaganda. While minorities are being taught race consciousness the white majority is instilled with a sense of guilt for these "wrongs" committed against minority groups. We are taught that consciousness of race is "un-American" and a manifestation of bigotry. We are told that all races are the same, and that we should discard the concept of race.

In this respect, all Jewish propaganda squares exactly with the communist line. There is a popular misconception to the effect that communism strives to set one race against another. This is a half-truth, which means it is more dangerous than a lie. The one thing communists fear more than anything else is a rebirth of race consciousness among the great white majority of the Christian world. The communists remember that the very instant the German people became race-conscious, they turned with deadly fury against Jewish-communism. They know the same thing could happen in this country. Therefore, all communist—and Jewish—propaganda is directed in an effort to destroy every vestige of race consciousness among the white people. That is what red propagandists seek to achieve with their propaganda movies and their "tolerance campaigns."

Communism vs Zionism

One other question must be discussed briefly. This concerns whether or not all Jews are communists. The answer is no. The reader will remember the earlier description of Communism and Zionism taking hold among the Jews of the Pale of Settlement as competitive movements after 1880. When the Bolsheviks took over Russia in 1917, they sought to impose their way of thinking on the entire Jewish population. As Jews, the Bolsheviks adhered to the belief that Jewish nationalism should be preserved, but they believed it should be orientated toward communism. The Communists regarded Zionism as an impractical scheme, wedded to British imperialism, and impossible of achievement. The Zionists, consisting of the more religious and orthodox Jews, stubbornly resisted this concept. As a result, the Communist Party established a special Jewish section to deal with the Zionists. They attempted, with only partial success to win over the children of the Ziorists by prohibiting the teaching of Zionism to children under twenty. Now before labeling this as "anti-Semitism," it should be remembered that these were measures imposed by one section of Jewry upon other Jews, and it should be remembered that Christians received no such preferential treatment.

This fight between Communists and Zionists has lasted right down to the present day. When the state of Israel was formed, tens of thousands of Zionists were permitted to emigrate from Russia and satellite territory to Palestine, in a move which still continues at this writing. (We should note that non-Jews are NEVER permitted to emigrate from

Communist Russia). But communist authorities have been exceedingly reluctant to permit young Jews to emigrate, and in many cases permission has been denied. Thus the fight continues. But the reader should remember that this is a fight between Jews. Whether Communists or Zionists, they still retain their Jewishness, and they stand united against all non-Jews. And although they travel different paths, both Communism and Zionism have the same common goal—domination of the world. Both work and plan for the day when the "chosen race" shall "inherit the earth."

Treason Update to 1994

Behind Communism takes us up to the time of the Alger Hiss case...and the execution of Atom bomb spies, Ethel and Julius Rosenberg on June 19, 1953. Since that time in the 1970's hundreds of thousands of pages of U.S. Government documents prove beyond a shadow of a doubt that the Rosenbergs were guilty. These documents were released as a result of the Rosenbergs' children's efforts, Robert and Michael Rosenberg. They now use the name Meeropol. Their son, Michael Meeropol Rosenberg is today—(1994)— an economics professor at Western New England College. The children have founded the *National Committee to Reopen the Rosenberg Case*. This is the face of the overwhelming evidence summed up in a 1983 book, ***The Rosenberg File—A Search for the Truth*** indicating that the Rosenbergs were in fact—guilty as charged.

Robert Meeropol Rosenberg

The Founding of Israel in 1948!

The successful launching of the nation state of Israel in 1948 brought an end to most of the Soviet spy activity. From that point on, the Communist/Zionist conspiracy had infiltrated the American government to such a degree that there was little need for the acquisition of technology by way of spying. It could simply be delivered through official channels from the United States government or through cooperating corporations to the Soviet Union. Still, one final major case was developed in 1957. KGB Col. Rudolph Abel was sentenced to 30 years on conspiracy to transmit atomic and military information to the Soviet Union. He was known as a 'master spy'

Rudolph Ivanovich Abel "master spy"

because he was the highest ranking espionage agent ever caught in this country.

His release was organized through the highest levels of the U.S. Government in cooperation with the pro-Zionist Communist Dwight David Eisenhower, who arranged for a flight by Francis Gary Powers in a famous U-2 plane mission to get photographs of the Soviet's missile sites. His flight data was leaked to the Soviet Union and he was shot down over Sverdiosk 1200 miles inside the Soviet border. Within months in February of 1962, Powers and Abel were swapped.

In the 1950's, plans to destabilize the United States through drug addiction were hatched and the importation by the CIA of heroin shipments on a massive scale was worked out with the CIA whose mission had already begun in Vietnam immediately after the war in 1945. John F. Kennedy's refusal to continue the Vietnam buildup was the primary reason for his assassination.

Nothing would be allowed to stand in the way of the drugging of U.S. servicemen in Vietnam and the use of the Vietnam buildup to cover for the importation of heroin in massive quantities by the U.S. Government and its co-opted agency, the CIA.

Prices paid for information by the KGB declined sharply after 1970!

Because of the penetration of the U.S. Government and the CIA was complete by the mid '50's, the prices paid for information by the KGB, declined sharply. For example, in 1985, the master spy John A. Walker was apprehended. He had sold top secret communications information to the Soviets for almost two decades but was never able to garner more than nominal amounts of money. He was joined in his efforts by his son, brother, and friends in espionage. The Soviets really didn't need the stolen data because of their control of the CIA.

John J. Walker on the night of his arrest.

In August of 1985 Vitaly Yurchenko one of the KGB's highest ranking officials walked from the Soviet Embassy in

Rome, Italy to the U.S. Embassy and asked for asylum. His defection, of course, was not real, as he knew that his agents were already in charge of the U.S. Government and the CIA. (Ronald Reagan had already suffered a bullet wound at the hand of a CIA manipulated friend of the Bush family and had thus been compromised.) Yurchenko told of two Americans who had betrayed the country. Both had

Vitaly Yurchenko

acute alcohol and drug problems and one was Ron Pelton who had been an employee of the National Security Agency and had informed the Russians that the U.S. had been able to place a tap on the communications cable in the Sea of Okhotsk and were able to monitor Soviet military communications. The Soviets promptly removed the tap.

Ron Pelton

The other Yurchenko tip off spy was Edward Lee Howard. The Howard Case illustrates the deep penetration of the CIA by the Mossad and the KGB, which routinely hired drug addicts and alcoholics. Howard had applied for a job for the CIA and when a polygraph test was given, he admitted to drugs and the spy agency hired him anyway.

Howard was assigned to Moscow, the CIA's most sensitive duty. Before he left, another polygraph showed that he had acute alcohol and drug problems. Then the CIA determined he was not fit to remain and he was fired. In 1983, he was left by the CIA with no source of income. In post termination CIA counseling, Howard admitted he had entertained the thoughts of selling secrets to the KGB to get revenge on the CIA. The CIA routinely refused to report the key information to the FBI, which is responsible for apprehending the spies caught by the CIA. Howard later escaped to the Soviet Union and

Edward Lee Howard

has never been head from. Yurchenko today is alive and well in Russia by simply walking away from a restaurant while under the CIA's control. Obviously here is proof positive that the CIA has been thoroughly penetrated at least as far back as the early '80's.

U.S.S.R. Deemed Useless—Secret Information passed directly to Israel!

The mid '80's saw the most revealing development in spying activity. From that time on, it became obvious that the Soviet Union was no longer of any importance to the World Jewish Conspiracy. From that time on, the data obtained through spying activities, rather than being passed through the front country (the USSR) was passed *directly to Israel*.

Jonathan Pollard

The most spectacular case of Mossad spying was that of Jonathan Pollard and his wife, who were both Jewish. He was convicted in 1985 and sentenced to life imprisonment primarily upon the statements provided to the sentencing judge by Secretary of Defense Caspar Weinberger, who also is Jewish. The Weinberger-Pollard matter is a classic example of how Jewish people can either be loyal to their native America or...in the case of Pollard...abandon all feelings of loyalty and goodwill toward the United States and transfer that loyalty to their homeland, the Marxist, Zionist, atheist state of Israel. Weinberger is an example (though rare) of a true Jewish patriot that Americans should always hold up as an example of how Jews should behave in the United States.

Caspar Weinberger

The Pollard case has resulted in unremitting vitriolic activity by the Jewish Zionist community to press for his early release. That effort continues up through the republication of *Behind Communism* in 1994 by Criminal Politics Book Club. Over the years, Pollard delivered, according to official government reports, *Tons* of secret documents to the Israeli Embassy in Washington D.C.

Included were U.S. satellite photos. The U.S. Government had politely provided Israel with substantial satellite photos of surrounding countries. Since this was deemed to be insufficient, the Mossad simply arranged to steal the satellite photos from the Unites States. Their agent was, of course, Jonathan Pollard.

Israel—NOT a close ally!

The Pollard spy case clearly reflects that Israel is not a friend or ally of the United States but an enemy. A close ally does not steal what it wants from its allies, but requests them through diplomatic channels and uses whatever political pressure it wishes to achieve its ends. Israel is well known for this kind of pressure. Obviously, as an enemy of the United States, Israel will use whatever illegal and treasonous means it has at its disposal to achieve its goals of total domination and submission of the United States.

Communism collapses—Iron Curtain destroyed 1989!

In 1990, the World Jewish Conspiracy was confident enough to simply do away with its secret offspring, the USSR. The USSR was no longer needed because of the total Jewish domination of the U.S. Government. The American people are now in bondage and the Soviet Union could be of much greater use to the world conspiracy as a prostrate forlorn country that needed the aid of the rest of the world. In the "prostrate" state, the USSR would be far more dangerous than an overt predator.

The end of the Zionist

Julius and Ethel Rosenberg

Sudoplatov

offspring, the USSR, has brought sensational memoirs of various Soviet spies. One of the most important so far was written by Pavel Sudoplatov, a KGB General. In his book, *Special Tasks*, he reveals how his department Spy Network thoroughly penetrated all the top secret atomic programs in the USA and Canada. Five of the top Marxists involved in the Manhattan project, which created the first atomic bomb, passed the information to Sudoplatov agents, Oppenheimer, Fermi, Gamov, Szilard, and Pontecarvo. The Rosenbergs, claims Sudoplatov, were only the small fry couriers.

Thanks to information provided by the above scientists, the Zionist conspiracy, was able to produce its own atomic weapons in the U.S.S.R. in under three years.

The memoirs also confirm earlier assertions that John Cairncross was the "fifth man" of the Cambridge Spy Ring... (including Anthony Blunt, Guy Burgess, Donald Maclean, and Kim Philby.) Oppenheimer, according to this book, was motivated by promises of the Soviet leaders to set up a post war Jewish state in the Crimea.

Agents in FDR's office!

Another bomb shell in the book is that Sudoplatov stated a Soviet GRU (military intelligence) officer told him he was running a controlled agent in President Franklin Roosevelt's office in addition to GRU agent Alger Hiss. (Hiss, by the way, is *still* fighting to prove his innocence.) Sudoplatov's wife was Jewish and Sudoplatov himself was ardently pro-Zionist. Most of the best agents were also Jews..."Under Stalin in the '30's," says Sudoplatov..."In every ministry at the time, Jews held top positions." He claims that from 1917 to 1948, Jews dominated Soviet intelligence and security services and spy networks in the USA. His book thus confirms—out of their own mouths—the highly accurate and perceptive research done by Frank L. Britton the original author of *Behind Communism*.

Epilogue!

Finally, the summary of this book must unfortunately rekindle claims that the world Jewry particularly of Marxist and Zionist persuasion were totally responsible for the Communist system that murdered 40 to 60 million people. Herein is the true "holocaust" that Americans should be concerned about. This is the "holocaust" that could be repeated here in America if enough of our citizens are not properly informed as to the dangerous regime in the entire history of the world:— *International Communism/Zionism*.

Jews takeover in Russia still celebrated in 1994

You may be surprised to know that on November 7, 1994—well after the Soviet Union supposedly ceased to exist—the Judaized Russians still celebrated the 77th Anniversary of the "Bolshevik" Revolution of 1917 by waving red Soviet flags and portraits of Stalin and Lenin. 30,000 people marched through Moscow to the KGB headquarters. The anniversary is a state holiday in what is now called the Confederation of Independent States. The "Soviet Union" never ceased to exist, and all planks of the Communist Manifesto are still enforced.

Lenin's Jewish Ancestry

Since this book was written it has been revealed that the most active leader of the Bolshevik Revolution, Vladimir Illyich Ulyanov, better known as Lenin (1870-1924), was of Jewish blood. Writing in the Broward Jewish Journal (2/25/92), Jesse

Zel Lurie states that the fact the Lenin "had Jewish grandparents is indisputable," and that "Lenin's Jewish ancestry is fully documented." Lurie further states:

> The documentary evidence was published recently in the Moscow News. It was largely ignored, for understandable reasons by the Jewish Media...The story of Lenin's heritage was discovered in the secret files of the Communist Party in Moscow. Lenin's grandfather, Alexander Blank, had been born to Jewish parents.

Lenin's Jewish ancestry was also revealed in the *London Jewish Chronicle* (April 21, 1995), when it did a review of a recently published biography of Lenin titled, Lenin: A New Biography, by Dmitri Volkogonov (The Free Press, 1994). The Article in the Jewish Chronicle stated:

> Volkogonov was able to come up with the fact that the founder of the Soviet state was the great-grandson of Moishe Itskovich Blank and the grandson of Srul Moishevich Blank. At his baptism, Blank changed his name and patronymic to Alekandr (Alexander) Dmitrievich.

> Lenin's Jewish origin on his maternal grandfather's side became, after his death, a matter of controversy between Lenin's sisters and Stalin. In a letter to Stalin, Anna, Lenin's elder sister, wrote: "It is probably no secret for you that the research on our grandfather shows that he came from a poor Jewish family."

Anna claimed that Lenin's "exceptional abilities" were a result of his Jewish heritage. She also state to Stalin that if Lenin's Jewish background was known, it would "serve in combating anti-Semitism." Stalin replied: "Not one word about it." The article further noted that Lenin "praised Jews in somewhat excessive terns, just as he was excessive in his denigration of (white) Russians." Lenin said that "the clever Russian is almost always a Jew or has Jewish blood in him."

Lenin also noted the Jews' greater "steadfastness as revolutionaries" compared to the white Russians. Lenin is often pictured in a side profile view to hide the Oriental feature of his eyes (see page 45). Lenin, Trotsky and Stalin all agreed that it was vital that Communism not appear as a Jewish scheme.

Lenin a Jew

On page 68 of this book, *Behind Communism*, author Frank Britton publishes a Soviet era poster showing that all of the founders of the Communist regime were Jews *except* Lenin.

When *Behind Communism* was first published, the official position of the U.S.S.R. was that Lenin was a Slavic Russian, not a Jew. However, subsequent to the book's publication, following the fall of the Iron Curtain in the mid-80s, it was finally admitted that, indeed, the monstrous criminal Vladimir Lenin, was a Jew!

The curator and director of the Lenin Museum has recently affirmed Lenin's Jewish ancestry. in July of 1991, the well known Jewish publication, *Jewish Chronicle*, also reported this fact. This means that Karl Marx, Moses Hess, Lenin, Trotsky, and virtually all Marxist/Communist founders were Jewish.

JEWISH CHRONICLE JULY 26 1991

Moscow magazine on Lenin's Jewish roots

BY ZEEV BEN-SHLOMO
EAST EUROPE CORRESPONDENT

Vladimir Ilyich Lenin, the creator of the Soviet Union, often officially praised as the embodiment of the Russian national genius, had a Jewish grandfather, according to the Moscow mass circulation weekly, Ogonyok.
There have been rumours to this

**For Additional Copies of
<u>Behind Communism</u>**
Send $18 (plus $5 s&h) to:
Power of Prophecy
1708 Patterson Road
Austin, Texas 78733
or call **Toll Free 1-800-234-9673**
or order from our website:
www.powerofprophecy.com

**Other related books of interest
available through Power of Prophecy:**

DNA Science and the Jewish Bloodline, by Texe Marrs (256 pages) $25 postpaid

Conspiracy of the Six-Pointed Star—Eye-Opening Revelation and Forbidden Knowledge About Israel, the Jews, Zionism, and the Rothschilds, by Texe Marrs (432 pages, large format) $30 postpaid

Protocols of the Learned Elders of Zion—The classic on International Zionism (325 pages) $25 postpaid

The Synagogue of Satan—The Secret History of Jewish World Domination, by Andrew Carrington Hitchcock (320 pages) $25 postpaid

Power of Prophecy
1708 Patterson Road
Austin, Texas 78733
or call **Toll Free 1-800-234-9673**
or order from our website:
www.powerofprophecy.com